BEAUTY & THE BEST

22 Stand Out Leaders
Share Their Experience, Challenges
And Best Advice
For Achieving Success
In The Beauty Industry

W&M

BEAUTY AND THE BEST

First published in February 2021

W&M Publishing

ISBN 978-1-912774-83-8 Pbk

ISBN 978-1-912774-82-1 eBk

Editors: Susan Routledge & Andrew Priestley

The rights of Susan Routledge, Katt Philipps, Verity Davies, Azra Riaz, Joan Scott, Marta Zaczkowska, Sarah Hurst, Jill Yvette Painter, Sara Shoemark, Clare Reed, Susan Over, Maria Mason, Brenda Kingswood, Catherine Whelan, Sarah Atkinson, Susanne Webb, Stefania Rossi, Jane Barker, Dawn Stanley, Anita Stubbings, Sandra Fludgate, and Lesley Blair to be identified as contributing authors of this work have been asserted in accordance with Sections 77 and 78 of the Copyright Designs and Patents Act, 1988.

A CIP catalogue record for this book is available from the British Library.

Contents

5 **Welcome To Beauty And The Best**

7 **Susan Routledge**
Reach For The Stars

15 **Katt Phillips**
Beauty Flourishes

23 **Verity Davies**
Carrying On The Legacy

31 **Azra Riaz**
My Parents Made My Struggle Their Own

39 **Joan Scott**
What If I Fall? But Oh Darling, What If You Fly?

49 **Marta Zaczkowska**
Life Is What You Make Of It

57 **Sarah Hurst**
I Grew My Business Organically

65 **Jill Yvette Painter**
REAL Dreams Are Worth Fighting For

75 **Sara Shoemark**
GLOW Is Teamwork

83 **Clare Reed**
The Road To Self-Satisfaction

91 **Susan Over**
Determination Is Definitely The Key To Success!

99 **Maria Mason**
The Mountains Of Life And Business

107 **Brenda Kingswood**
I Had A Dream

115 **Catherine Whelan**
Embracing Life's Challenges

123 **Sarah Atkinson**
Yes! This Is Working!

131 **Susanne Webb**
Reach For The Moon But Aim For The Stars

139 **Stefania Rossi**
Dare To Dream

147 **Jane Barker**
This Is Me

155 **Dawn Stanley**
Thirty Years And Counting

163 **Anita Stubbings**
Always Believe In Yourself

171 **Sandra Fludgate**
Changing Lives!

177 **Lesley Blair**
Never Be Afraid To Dream Big

185 **About Beauty Directors Club Community**

187 **Would You Like To Contribute
To Future Editions Of Beauty And The Best?**

Welcome To Beauty And The Best

The Beauty Industry is a fabulous multi-billion ever growing, ever evolving global industry.

My experience has always been that it is filled with the most amazing individuals, each creating and carving their career paths and with never two journeys ever the same.

I feel totally privileged to be the instigator able to bring together this book, highlighting some of the amazing opportunities that this great Industry has to offer by showcasing the highs, lows and fantastic stories behind 22 amazing beauty industry leaders.

Their journeys span across many years, many continents and many cultural backgrounds.

This book contains no cherry-picked authors, instead it is filled with truly passionate leaders who answered a call to inspire, by giving an honest insight into their intimate business and life journeys with gems of advice sprinkled in every story.

Our combined aim and never waning passion is to inspire other fellow Beauty Industry Professionals, our fantastic clients who make our working days such a pleasure, plus the next generations embarking into this fabulous and varied career.

I have had the absolute pleasure to have been closely associated with each and every author either as personal business consultancy clients, members of *Beauty Directors Club* or close associates.

My most favourite motivational quote ever is:

Whether You Think You Can… Or You Think You Can't,
You're Right.

Henry Ford

As you read through these stories, *The Can Do* and forward thinking attitude of these open and honest Beauty Leaders jumps out from every page, overcoming so many hurdles and never compromising their total professionalism, no matter what life and the economic climate throws at us.

On behalf of us all, we hope you enjoy this inspirational read.

Susan Routledge

Reach for The Stars

Susan Routledge

All I can ever remember wanting, was to be in the beauty industry.

From being very small I loved the thought enhancing someone's looks with my hand-me- down cosmetics collection, much to the horror of any visitors (victims!) who came to my home, and then dared to linger for any length of time.

I was really timid as a child, but I was brought up by the perfect parents for me.

My Mother, the perfect homemaker who truly believed I could be and do anything. My Father, a hard-working foreman Joiner by day and a property developer entrepreneur by night, and every weekend.

As a teenager my parents divorced, but I saw this as a bonus, not a negative, as I now had dedicated time to spend with my Dad without the family tensions. It was time often collecting rents, but it was still quality time to me.

My Dad's strategy was to work like crazy, make as many

property investments as possible and then to retire early at 55, and live off the profits.

So, the fact that I wanted to go to college to study Beauty Therapy and Hairdressing, which back in the late 1970s was a four-year course, seemed totally crazy to him.

The nearest courses were hundreds of miles away… but then, as I was due to leave school, a course opened up in my region and I knew I had to be on it.

I didn't have a clue what I wanted to do by the end. I just thought I would figure that out later, after all I had four years to think about it.

As the course drew to a close, I had increasing pressure from my Dad to find a job.

Any decent jobs were miles away, so I decided my best option was to start a beauty and hairdressing freelancing business without initially telling my Dad.

So, with flyers in hand, my Mum and I spent a full day posting leaflets out. To my total surprise, the hallway telephone was ringing by the time we got back. So, I started the next day, with my Morris Marina car packed and ready to visit my first clients and with my Mum at home as my makeshift receptionist.

I became so busy so quickly. There were only two things wrong: about 95% of my clients wanted hairdressing services as beauty certainly hadn't caught on in my small town; and, I was working ridiculous hours, as I didn't want to let anyone down or to turn anyone away.

My Dad, by now had found out and offered to help me with my book-keeping but I decided to keep my success under wraps until I could unequivocally prove my achievements to him. I had this vision of sitting him down at the table, opening my amazing accounts book and my Dad being so, so proud.

That day never came.

On an early February night, my Dad went to bed and never woke up again. He was only 50. He had a huge cerebral haemorrhage which instantly ended his life.

It just didn't seem real. I just couldn't take it in.

I had driven past my Dad the day before. He was up a ladder and looked busy and I certainly didn't have time to stop as I was racing to my next appointment. I just thought I would see him later.

I didn't know what to do. I wanted to just run away, but I had all of my clients to see. Cancelling them just meant a longer wait list, so I did what I thought my Dad would expect me to do and carried on working as much as I could.

I started to resent the business I had created. I resented that it was so demanding, that I had no free time, and that it had stopped me chatting to my Dad on that last day of his life. I resented that I hadn't had chance to show him my accounts book. I resented everything, including that it wasn't even the career that I wanted. I realised that I just wanted to prove to my Dad I could do it, and now I was trapped in it all.

I now firmly believe that the universe will always correct things, and although no-one could bring my Dad back, I believe that there are external forces helping us.

Within weeks of my Dad's death, I developed a really severe rash over all of my hands. I had always protected my hands with gloves whilst working, but this rash came out of the blue and I started reacting to everything associated with hair products. It was so painful that it would make me cry. I was so low anyway, but just putting this happy face on for the world.

My GP told me that I must look for another career. It was a relief, but I also had so many clients and responsibilities, but I knew I couldn't go on. By now this business had no meaning to me and I literally just gave my whole business away to another local stylist.

Over the next couple of years, I took on retail jobs. I just wanted minimum responsibility and time to heal. I stumbled upon a book by Louise Hay called, *You Can Heal Your Life*. I was so fascinated, and this started my never-ending journey in self-development.

By now the Beauty Industry was gaining momentum and I decided to take some refresher courses and start all over again.

I now had a clear vision and total belief that I was on the right path for ME, and nothing was going to stop me.

I started freelancing again, but this time just in beauty therapy, and also got a position teaching in a private college one day a week.

Within exactly one year, I opened Finishing Touch Clinic, in my hometown, as a small salon. I then purchased premises, and with gradual expansion, we became the largest Beauty Salon in my region and one of the largest in the UK.

I wrote myself a note declaring that my salon would win the title of *Professional Beauty Best Large UK Beauty Salon*. It was a really big ask as previous winners all seemed to be well known city centre salons and my business was unknown and 14 miles from any city.

We proudly won the title in 2007. And this was the start of over 12 National Business Awards and many other business accolades.

I have always created amazing teams around me, and I systemised the business to work independently of me.

This worked perfectly as it gave my team a chance to develop further. I always support my team to follow their dreams and keep in touch with nearly all, who are now spread as far as Australia. I am so proud that for a period of over 25 years, we never lost a therapist to another salon.

We have a constant staff training and development programme, which freed my time to avidly travel to develop advanced business skills from some of the world's top entrepreneurs.

I was being constantly asked for advice from other salon owners on how they could successfully grow their salon and win national awards too.

Amongst giving so much free advice, I also became fascinated with how two salons could look totally the same on the surface, yet one would be flourishing, whilst the other was failing.

I invested heavily in a totally unique programme working closely for a year with a global business turnaround expert and a small team of four other entrepreneurs, learning first-hand skills, transforming the fortunes of distressed businesses. What I learnt was invaluable.

I perfected a business formula that would transform a

salon business of any size or condition and trademarked my formula. From here onwards, I have had the great pleasure of still owning my salon, with a fantastic team and wonderful clients, many who have been with us over 30 years.

I also have the pleasure to work as an International Business Consultant and work on a daily basis with so many fantastic beauty business owners within *Beauty Directors Club*.

I am blessed to attract the best clients and the most amazing network of people to work with.

My love is helping others to Reach for The Stars too and it makes me so proud when they achieve their greatest goals.

Along my business journey, I have created my own personal formula to Reach for The Stars on an analogy of LIFE which I would love to share with you.

- **The L is for LOVE.** I always aim to only do what I love.
  I send love daily to myself plus everyone and everything.
  In return I only attract the best people to me, without fail.

- **The I is for INVEST.** I invest time and energy in myself on a daily
  basis. I meditate every day and spend time learning, journaling,
  and visualising what I want to create. I have a never-ending
  thirst for personal and business development.

- **The F is for FOCUS.** I only focus forwards and in a positive way.
  I believe everything happens for a reason, giving us emotional
  feedback and an opportunity to think better thoughts.
  I don't ever dwell in negativity as it keeps you stuck and attracts
  more of the same.

- **The E is for EXPECT.** This is a huge one. You can only
  create what you truly believe.

I believe that I can create anything that anyone else has achieved, and you can too.

My true wish for you, is to live a fantastic life created by yourself, for yourself.

Reach for The Stars!

About Susan Routledge

Susan Routledge is a Multi Award Winning Salon Owner, International Business Consultant and trusted Industry Advisor. Susan has been in the Beauty Industry for over 35 years and is recognised in the Top 100 UK Industry Influencers for her passion and dedication. She is also part of the Professional Board for BABTAC helping to represent and raise industry standards for the Beauty Industry. Her down to earth, light-hearted approach has made her an International Speaker and an established Awards Judge.

Susan is the founder of her trademarked STABLE business formula, author of *The Little Book of Client Retention* and best seller co-author of *Your Best Life and* has an online business turnaround programme called *Salon Success Freedom*. She is also the creator of *Beauty Directors Club*, an ever-growing global membership and close community for salon, clinic and spa business owners with resources and multi expert advice. Susan's online blog, *Beauty Entrepreneurs*, has attracted over 7,000 global subscribers for her weekly hints, tips and insights.

Contact Susan

http://susanroutledge.com

http://beautydirectorsclub.com

https://www.facebook.com/groups/beautyentrepreneurshub

Beauty Flourishes

Katt Philipps, LE MUA

I was raised in a small town in South Carolina. My parents were two highly accomplished, extraordinary people in their own rights. My mother was an Audrey Hepburn look-alike, so it was no surprise she was a former Halston model, not to mention a world-class equestrian. My father retired as a naval officer and became a successful surgeon. As for me, I inherited my father's appearance, with strong German features but thankfully no beard!

My father believed all things should be unisex. Things that were strictly *for girls* to be a waste of time. Femininity was frowned upon and regarded as frivolous and unnecessary. As most little girls do, I wanted to please my dad, so I pushed dolls aside in favor of math, science, and engineering.

But my mother and I had a fun little secret. We would make our way to one of the most unimaginable places for my father: the beauty counter at the local department store. By age six, it had become my *happy place*. It was the one place my mother would have us dress for, and I always felt so glamorous when I went inside. The ladies at the makeup counter would give me a little lipstick and sometimes, if I was lucky, a bit of eye shadow! With that, a beauty addict was born! *"Just be sure to wash it off before your dad comes home,"* my mom would say about the makeup from our secret outings to the salon counter.

As I grew older, my teenage angst had strained the relationship between me and my mother to the point that our only common language was in the potions and lotions we both loved. It sometimes seemed the only place where we could see eye-to-eye was at that beauty counter. When we were together there, we both loved feeling like we were being transported out of our small town to the stylish big city.

However, our jaunts suddenly came to a sudden end when my mother was diagnosed with a rare breast cancer. She began chemotherapy the same day I graduated from high school and urged me to start my adult life as she began her battle. Wanting to reconnect with her, I would pore over magazines trying to find products to help her feel more like herself. As her cancer raged, she lost all her hair and gained surgical scars and radiation tattoos. I never heard her complain.

Strong and stoic, she never seemed to falter until the day she broke down as I stood behind her in the mirror. *"Look at me. I look like I am in a concentration camp."* Her shoulders went limp as she sobbed. I could feel her giving up. Beauty, at that moment, was no longer about pretty packaging and feeling glamorous. Beauty was about seeing who she felt like on the inside reflected in the mirror. She could no longer see herself.

Three weeks later, she was gone.

Still haunted by the experience and my mother's vulnerability, I started college. Obsessed with understanding how the mind and appearance were interconnected, I studied philosophy, psychology, and sociology. I never wanted anyone to feel like my mother did that day looking in the mirror. I was determined to find a way to overcome it. After graduation, however, my studies had left me with more questions than answers, so I did what anyone would -- I moved to Hollywood.

With my mom still in mind, I studied beauty, wig making, and special effects. I began working toward a career as a film and television makeup artist, perfecting the art of making people feel beautiful. I soaked up all the tips and tricks I could find, all the little intricacies that made stars look extraordinary. I wanted to learn how to paint a happy face on someone sad. I wanted to paint *healthy* on someone *sick*.

Once I started working in Hollywood, I quickly got swept up in the glamour of film. I loved meeting famous people and zipping from set to set. Every day was a new adventure, and even though the hours were long and grueling, I loved bouncing between making stuntmen into monsters and putting beautiful makeup on a star. The speed of it all had almost silenced my mother's words of sadness. At this point, I only wanted to drown them out completely with other noise. I kept working, stacking my plate higher and higher. Movies, parties, events - my new focus was only to make a name for myself!

Make a name I did. I built a reputation for being able to work with some of the most difficult actors in Hollywood. Repeat bookings became more frequent, and as a result, some actors became personal friends. This wasn't always a good thing, as professional lines began to blur and I was exposed to the underbelly of the Hollywood lifestyle. The makeup artist dream I had been chasing dissolved into helping actors hide eating disorders and crippling anxiety. Beauty was a mask to hide behind, and I had become the enabler.

On the brink of a breakdown from the weight of the truths I was carrying, I turned to charity work. I volunteered to bring children of rival gangs together through makeup. Kids from both sides of the firing line worked together they painted each other while sharing the stories of the violence of their neighborhoods. Their reality was in stark contrast to the rest of Hollywood. Together we learned to cover the scars of past wounds and looked forward to building a better future. Beauty became a platform for understanding, allowing a community to form where there was none.

The kids taught me more about humanity than I had taught them about makeup. When the school closed, the career that had led me to them no longer felt right. I loved the journey while I was in Hollywood, but I wanted a return to making people feel beautiful without all the smoke and mirrors of a film set. For me, beauty had become about empowerment again, and Hollywood had nothing left for me.

I was starting from scratch. I knew I wanted to be rooted in a community again rather than continually having to re-introduce myself to strangers. It was scary to start over in my 30s, but the small-town values I knew when I was a child were alive and well in the Midwest, and that's where I chose to reinvent myself.

While I had underestimated what it would take to start over (and being in a new area didn't make it any easier),

I had chosen to leave everything behind even as I was climbing to the height of my career. I knew my heart was pulling me someplace else. I decided instead of putting makeup on people, I would focus on taking it off. I had no experience when I switched to aesthetics, but I still heard my mom's words in the back of my head, and I was eager to learn new lessons in beauty.

I centered my practice around seeing a healthy reflection in the mirror, knowing that it was vital to feeling healthy. Initially, I set my sights on medical aesthetics. Patients would come in, tell us what they didn't like about their appearance, and we would fix it. We would see the same patients come back, each time wanting more and more work done. After a few months, my heart became heavy, and I knew I needed to keep searching.

I moved on to a busy hair salon and spa, and at first felt like I had landed in the right place. The spa was beautiful, with multiple rooms and busy therapists. It gave me the same excited feeling as walking up to the beauty counter with my mother when I was a girl. The doors regularly flooded with customers and my bookings skyrocketed. I loved being in the treatment room and quickly started training new aestheticians and speaking at trade shows for the salon.

As I moved up in the company, however, I could see things changing. Management focus went from client care to ranking clients based on how much money they could bring. Profit was always top of the back-of-house conversation which was in stark contrast to the personal nature of the work we performed. The time spent with the clients felt like the antithesis of what was being said by the company.

I knew there had to be another way.

It was a mixed blessing when that spa location closed, and I took it as a sign that it was now time to start my journey as an entrepreneur. Back in the Hollywood scene, people found their own networks and outlets for satisfying heart and maintaining integrity, and I was determined to do the same. With meager funds scraped together, I opened my own skincare clinic in 2013.

I sat up night after night, thinking about what I had learned along the way. What lessons would I bring to the center of my business? I'd realized that beauty is the embodiment of how we see ourselves. Beauty can be empowering or make us vulnerable. I had learned that with love and understanding, beauty flourishes.

With this in mind, I set out to create a safe space that allowed others to be their authentic selves without judgment from the world around them. I made my business choices purely on what was in the client's best interest. I set out to treat each person as if there were to be with me for the rest of my life. Within months of opening, my books were full, and I even had my first international clients crossing borders to get their facials. With a heart-focused center, my clinic continues growing to this day, despite a year-long waitlist.

This has been my journey. There's no single big secret to my success, except realizing that you must remain true to your personal integrity and always lead with love and understanding.

About Katt Philipps

After 28-years in the Industry, Spa Owner and Licensed Aesthetician Katt Philipps has studied beauty from almost every angle. Katt's first career as a Hollywood makeup artist inspired her love of all things skin. Her passion for people, relationships, business and education allowed her to work in salon and medical spas before opening and building her bustling private multi six-figure skin clinic in Chicago.

Katt has continued to grow her business with a passion for improving the world around her. With her husband Brian, Katt has continued to grow her business online using retail to bring awareness to different charities by donating a portion of every sale to a new charity every quarter.

Katt's busy beauty studio in the Chicago suburbs continues to be her source of inspiration. Along with multiple international beauty industry podcasts and forums, Katt has appeared on CNN, BBC, and in *Forbes Magazine*. Katt hopes her newest project, *The Beauty Educator*, will serve as a resource for other beauty professionals to flourish in a changing market.

Contact Katt

Hello@thebeautyeducator.com

www.grafinskin.com

www.thebeautyeducator.com

Instagram @the.beauty.educator

Carrying On The Legacy

Verity Davies

There is no such word as *can't!*

To this day, those words continually ring in my ears. My Grandmother, Mary Haworth would always repeat them to me. I used to think, here she goes again. But that was before I realised what an amazing lady she really was. Unfortunately, she had passed away before I truly appreciated what she meant.

I am one of Mary Haworth's four grandchildren. As children, my Grandmother would visit us usually every Tuesday, always armed with treats and books - either on self-help or positive thinking. We never read them! She loved nothing more than to leave these books wherever she went, in the hope they would change somebody's life. She was a positive thinker and doer, definitely born before her time.

Having been put into the workhouse age four and then fostered from there, life did not start out easy for her. Fortunately, she went on to marry a solicitor and had my father. But sadly, at just 46 years old, her husband died. Mary, however, was never one to give up, and in the wake of my Grandfather's death she made the bold decision to follow her dreams, she took herself off to London, and enrolled at the Delia Collins School of Beauty. At this time there were very few colleges that taught beauty. Here, she qualified in Electrolysis, Massage, Facials, Manicures and Pedicures and even the chemistry of how to make her own products. But it was electrolysis that was her passion. Once qualified, she returned to her hometown of Ashton-under-Lyne and opened her own salon. Mary Haworth Beauty Culture was born 1st August 1955.

Mary was a pioneer of her times: she had an enviable foresight and enough determination to build up a business in a world where the odds were stacked against her. Many thought she was crazy, and it couldn't work.

How wrong were they!

While in Mary's day, beauty salons were a rare sight, today every town and most villages have a beauty salon. Today, her legacy continues in the same spot in Ashton-under-Lyne. In fact, we have never been able to confirm if there are any salons still running that are older than Mary Haworth Beauty Culture in the UK or the world for that matter!

Mary worked initially on her own, gradually building her business, but it wasn't long before she needed help. So, she began training others, this enabled her to grow her business with her newly qualified students. She maintained a very strict professional demeanour: when in the salon, everybody would call her Mrs Haworth and she commanded the greatest respect from all the girls she employed. The salon was a very private quiet place, everybody talked in a very quiet whisper.

Mary retired at the age of 70, but not before she had ensured her eldest granddaughter, my sister Suzanne, had qualified and was able to continue running the business. I followed Suzanne into the business eight years later.

Since its launch in 1955, Mary Haworth Beauty Culture has constantly evolved, responding to 65 years of changes and developments in the beauty industry. We have innovated with the times, bringing in laser treatments, semi-permanent makeup and specialised facials – the list goes on. We have had a number of salon refits and expanded our premises as our customer base and treatments grew.

Even the way we work has developed. When the salon first opened, Mary had no beauty suppliers to go to for equipment, these had to be sourced from medical suppliers, and her furniture needed to be custom made. Today we are supported by a thriving network of vendors and suppliers helping us to keep maintain state-of-the-art services. As a result, first, second, and third generations of families continue to patronise the salon.

Mary Haworth died in 1997, aged 90.

I would like to think she was proud of us both and grateful that we have continued her legacy – both in keeping the salon running to this day, but also in being brave and investing in the latest beauty technologies and treatments. Both Suzanne and I have now worked in the business longer than Mary herself.

I never had the pleasure of working alongside my Grandmother, as she had retired before my time. But through her, and through my own career experiences I have taken away three key lessons on how to succeed in this industry: seeking advice and support from peers is invaluable; clients want an experience, not just a service; and always trust your intuition.

I decided to embark on a career in beauty when I was 20, so with my Grandmother's blessing, I enrolled at Lillian Maund School of Beauty, which was in Stockport at the time. Here I was given great training to a very high standard. Everything had to be impeccable: strictly all white uniforms, tights and flat shoes worn in the salon and a navy-blue coat and navy court shoes that had to be worn travelling to and from the college. Hair had to be short or tied back and full makeup always worn. Nails were never visible beyond the end of the fingertips and were checked before entering any practical lesson. We did look amazing and were easily identifiable.

Oh, to have those standards again!

After qualifying I began working alongside my sister, Suzanne. I was very lucky. While my journey in beauty had just begun, I was starting out in a ready-made, successful business of 30 years at the time. As sisters we work well together, as we are so different. Not long after I joined the business, Suzanne went on maternity leave with her daughter and so I was thrust head first into the day-to-day running of the salon.

I quickly built up my clientele. I had limitless energy in those days and didn't know when to say no to clients. In retrospect, I probably allowed the business to grow too quickly and became a victim of my own success, it was all work and no play. The business had doubled in size, but I didn't really have the skills to manage our growing team.

My advice to myself at 23 years old would be slow down and seek advice from others in the industry. At that time there weren't mentor groups, thank goodness times have changed. I realise now that support is key to running a successful business. Often, I would have sleepless nights worrying about the business, but my motto now is: *There are no problems, just solutions*. It wasn't until I had my second son that I allowed myself time to develop away from the salon. As I became a mother, my mindset veered closer to my grandmother's, and I aspired to take a more holistic approach to my work and life.

My journey is one that continues to unfold to this day. Following the road of holistic therapy has changed my whole view of beauty.

In my younger days I didn't understand how important the word therapist was. Now, being a beauty specialist who provides an experience, not just a treatment, keeps me motivated to continue and grow in what I really love. I have been lucky to qualify in holistic therapies of Reflexology, Aromatherapy, Manual Lymphatic Drainage, Indian Head Massage and many other shorter courses. All my tutors were really inspiring, and each course catapulted me onto the next. I believe a successful career in beauty is one of constant learning and growth, and this should shine through to your customers. I am proud to see my clients leaving the salon knowing I have given them my best, and this probably separates me from those who spend a short time in this career and those like myself who spend a lifetime in this industry.

Finally, I have also learnt the importance of intuition.

For me, this happened when being taught reflexology. During the course, my tutor would say: '*You will know when an area needs extra treatment.*' At first, I really didn't understand what she meant by this. The *light bulb moment* didn't come to me until I was actually with a client and, indeed, it began to happen. Now I love following my own intuition whilst in treatments and sometimes I just listen to my inner self. It comes up with some great advice, it can even surprise me, let alone some of the people I have shared it with!

During the time I have worked in beauty I have had the pleasure of working with some incredible therapists, many of whom I have kept in touch with and I have had the pleasure of seeing them grow their own businesses. I never see them as competition as I always try to look at the bigger picture. There are clients for every salon, if you work hard, have high standards and give your best, clients will find you.

Like many business owners, 2020 stretched me to the limit and the pandemic became the most stressful time in all my years in beauty. I was fortunate to have enrolled in Susan Routledge Beauty Directors Club, and this proved to be invaluable, in that it gave me support from other salon owners going through exactly what I was going through with lots of help and ideas of how to handle these unprecedented times. I am most grateful for this group of people who under normal circumstances I might never have met.

Let's hope salon owners engage with each other more, because as an industry together we are most definitely stronger.

About Verity Davies

Verity Davies is a Company Director and practising therapist at Mary Haworth Beauty Culture in Ashton-under-Lyne, Greater Manchester.

Verity has over 36 years of experience in the beauty industry, having joined Mary Haworth after qualifying from the Lillian Maund School of Beauty. Since then, Verity has developed a wide range of expertise and qualifications, including advanced Electrolysis in Thread Vein and Skin Tag Removal, a range of holistic therapies, Semi-permanent Makeup, and Meso Therapy.

Through affiliations to Espa, Environ, CACI and Jessica, Verity keeps abreast of new products and innovations in the industry, and continually develops her craft through additional training, something she see's as essential.

As well as maintaining a full portfolio of clients, Verity is also responsible for the company's management and development, including stakeholder and supplier relations, accounts management and finance, staff recruitment, welfare and professional development.

Contact Verity Davies

verity@maryhaworth.co.uk

http://maryhaworth.co.uk

https://m.facebook.com/maryhaworthbeauty/

http://www.instagram.com/maryhaworth1955/

Beauty And The Best

My Parents Made My Struggle Their Own

Azra Riaz

Growing up in an Asian family in Yorkshire in the 1980s meant that big life decisions, and the pathways to make them happen, were limited. Career opportunities for women like me were often influenced by a conservative community mindset. Risks were discouraged and independent thinking was frowned upon. I wasn't the type of girl who could go along with this, but not just because I felt rebellious.

In high school, I was preparing for a career in law when, after a two-week placement at a solicitor's firm, I realised an office environment was not for me. I felt suffocated and trapped without a creative outlet. I wanted a career and job that I would love to get up for and go to every day.

I thought about this carefully before realising that my creativity flowed most when I was practicing hair styles and makeup ideas on my sisters. It was something I stumbled into, teaching myself by looking at photos and then trying to replicate them.

Getting family and friends ready for weddings became a ritual.

I sat down with my parents and told them I didn't want to do a law degree but a hair and beauty course instead. I also needed £370 for the books and equipment. After listening to me patiently, my father left the room and returned with a cheque for the course. I had to be 17 to start it so I continued with my Law A-levels that year as a thank you to my parents.

Then, at 17, I enrolled on a three-year hair and beauty course at the local college. I loved every minute. In my final year, I completed a week's placement at Glemby, a prestigious salon within Rackhams, a city centre department store.

They soon offered me a Saturday job which became full time after my course. By the end of my first year, I was the national runner-up Sothys Girl of the Year. It was a dream working in a store of that calibre and an amazing feeling knowing others recognised my potential and talent.

Whilst working, I was approached by my college Head who encouraged me to go into teaching. Juggling work with a part time teaching course was stressful, but I did so well that the college offered me a lecturer position.

On my first day as a lecturer at 21 years old, I found my class lined up outside the lecture room. As I opened the door and walked in, two cleaners shouted across the room, *"You can't come in here unless your lecturer is with you."*

"I AM the lecturer," I told them.

As they apologised, I overheard them saying *she looks too young to be a lecturer.* Standing in front of all my students, I could have felt intimidated or empowered by them.

I felt the latter because I believed in myself and knew I had the knowledge, the experience and qualifications that my students needed from me.

At my job, I worked my way up quickly to Beauty Manageress, absorbing the leadership qualities it gave me. Achieving something I never thought I would be in the running for changed my mindset. It stirred a passion and hunger for success. I knew I wanted more than just to work in a salon. I wanted my own salon.

By age 23, I found myself signing the documents to purchase a business property with my father. The fact that it was a former butcher's shop, closed for some 20 years and needing gutting, wasn't an obstacle to me. It was an ideal location on one of the main roads into the city centre. It was a place I could redesign and call my own.

By this time, news had spread through the community about my choice of career and it raised a few eyebrows, particularly since everyone thought I was going to be studying law. But in time, I discovered the same people who were giving my parents so much grief were then encouraging their daughters to careers in hair and beauty due to the success I had achieved. Some of them would even seek work placement opportunities for their daughters at my salon.

It was full steam ahead after that (as my father, who was in the navy, would say) and my salon grew from strength to strength. My sister soon completed a hair and beauty course and came to join me. We became a dream team, winning Salon of Excellence awards and being featured both in an ITV documentary and on BBC Look North.

Competing in the L'Oréal colour trophy, we were

introduced to legendary stylist Andrew Collinge, which inspired us greatly. We travelled up and down the country attending exhibitions, leaving our clients waiting to see excitedly what treatment we would launch next.

Another proud moment for both my father and ourselves was meeting the late Benazir Bhutto who, at the time, was the Prime Minister of Pakistan. We had a wonderful and inspirational conversation together. She told me to *Never doubt yourself as a woman. We can achieve everything once you put your mind to it. Believe in yourself and others will believe in you too.* Such true words.

When you start believing in yourself and you have a good positive mindset, good opportunities all come your way and like-minded people become part of your journey. The power we each have within us is the belief that we can and will succeed, even when the stakes are against you. Be the one to lead and let others follow. Sometimes this means having to educate society through your example, which is what I had done without realising. Without thinking about it, I had become that pioneer and role model.

That wouldn't have been possible without having the best parents ever, parents that believed in me and wanted me to succeed. My father, in particular, gave me self-belief, passion, confidence and the determination I needed. Later in life, I realised that these attributes became the foundations to my business and my leadership abilities.

Now that my salon has been established for almost 30 years, my story isn't finished. We have since expanded by merging into the shop next door and totally rebranding. We're ready to expand further, building on the many lessons I've learned.

For example, beauty therapists are all amazing at what they do, but sometimes lack the business management acumen needed to stay afloat. In my case, a business course certainly helped. A successful business is more than providing a great service or even a fantastic customer experience. It's about managing expectations about finances and how you treat staff so that the hard work you put in is protected from unwanted surprises. It's about sharing your vision with others.

For me, this meant actively networking with others and letting my positivity attract like-minded business people. This is key to reaching the next level. As you begin to share ideas – I have used an ideas journal recently – you'll see that your self development journey creates enthusiasm amongst your staff and a more positive work environment. I'm always looking at what course to do next or what book is best to read because you never stop learning in our industry.

My father recently passed away and, although I was heartbroken, I was happy he saw how his support and encouragement for me changed my life immeasurably. In his memory, I have no choice but to get back up and focus again. He knew that my capabilities in running a successful business kept changing and improving because of the determination I had within me.

I am constantly thinking about how to improve the business and myself. I never switch off, I'm always on the go, my mind never sleeps. And I'm loving every minute of it.

Now, I'm having my best years ever. By setting goals in an organised way, with a chart on my office wall, I'm able to focus on what needs to be done. I'm supported by an amazing team who have helped build the brand and achieve my dreams. I have taken time to build a better work life balance, making time to support my children and mother, who has never stopped supporting me with her words of wisdom and love.

This includes a decision to go back into part time teaching. I've completed my Cert Ed equivalent qualifications at the local university and am now half way through my assessors' award. I would love to help continue to inspire people into our industry.

After all these years and with a wealth of knowledge under my belt, I've realised that, just like taking your driving test, you are taught to pass the test before you learn to drive. In our industry, I was spending time educating newly qualified staff to work in real salon environment when they should have been able to come out of college qualified with this knowledge in the first place.

Ultimately, passion makes any business work and your personality is what brings in the clients. I can honestly say I have the best clients who have supported me throughout my years in business. They've become more like friends and it's an honour to be there for them too.

You can't stop investing in them and I'll always look after them. Just like my parents invested in and looked after me.

About Azra Riaz

Azra Riaz is an experienced stylist, beauty therapist, and qualified lecturer in hair and beauty. Her salon Libertes was established in 1992 in response to the needs of the local hair and beauty market. Her pioneering concept made Libertes the go to salon for the Asian hair and beauty sector and beyond.

As word spread, Libertes soon established itself as a leader in Yorkshire and further afield. Azra has continued to be single minded in her vision to provide the very best in hair and beauty since embarking on her career. She combines confidence with creativity, experimentalism with dexterity and charisma with business acumen.

Amongst its many accolades, Libertes has achieved a five-star *Salon of Excellence* status in the *Good Salon Guide*. Azra has served as Beauty Editor for *Roop Magazine* and has been featured in several other publications including *Asian Bride* magazine. She has also appeared in documentaries for ITV and BBC *Look North*.

Contact Azra

info@libertes.co.uk

www.libertes.co.uk

https://www.facebook.com/libertes.bradford

https://www.instagram.com/libertes.bradford

What If I Fall? But Oh Darling, What If You Fly?*

Joan Scott

I was blessed to grow up surrounded by sheep, dogs and hills. Perhaps not the usual background for a career in beauty, but perfect for helping me develop a grounded, balanced approach to life, an appreciation for farming, plus a lifelong love of sheepdogs!

At the age of 11, after toying with the idea of becoming a nurse, I found a book called *Beauty Culture...* and wow, it looked like a dream career! This beauty *culture* looked magical and I so wanted to be part of it. Growing up in a quiet little village in Cumbria, I knew there was a huge exciting world out there, but I didn't think I would make the break and escape the hills.

At junior school I developed a love of competitions, maybe it was because I was shy and lacking in confidence, and competitions rewarded you for trying your absolute best. Competition success made you feel amazing, your confidence soared as you had recognition that your work was good. My competitive streak led me to becoming a bit of a

Blue Peter badge groupie, getting two traditional ones, a silver one and even stalking the BBC to ask how I could get a gold one. Apparently, these were only awarded to children who had saved someone from drowning or rescued people from a house fire. I'm sad to say I was plotting how I could do this!

My plan was to be a makeup artist, so at 18 I moved to Manchester to study Hair and Beauty. This was quite a big step for me, but I had no choice if I wanted to follow my dream career. I aimed to get qualified and then pursue my ambition to be a makeup artist in TV and films, initially maybe at the BBC. And then Hollywood would surely beckon?

I absolutely loved the course. I never had a moments regret. I really enjoyed the anatomy and physiology classes; it was so factual and science-based and underpinned all the spa treatments we studied. My other love was the creative side; the makeup classes, especially the full-body makeup.

During the course we had the opportunity to enter makeup competitions, which I embraced fully. I was lucky to win the high-profile makeup competition in my final year, which increased my confidence and helped me to believe in myself. Again, competitions helped me to step out of my comfort zone and challenge myself to do better, which then helped give me the confidence to apply to the BBC to be a makeup artist, what could possibly go wrong?

My plan then took a tumble, unfortunately, the BBC weren't taking any makeup artists on that year. I was gutted and had to quickly find a way to stay in Manchester, if not, I'd have to head back to the Cumbrian hills and become a sheepdog trainer (or use my new grooming skills and open a poodle parlour!)

So, slightly panicking, I applied for a role as a Physiotherapy Assistant, which was frightening, and I thought I'd blown my career in beauty. I hadn't yet learned to rely on the bigger plan that life has mapped out for all of us.

If I'd known then, what I know now, I would have relaxed and enjoyed the detour. Instead, I was anxious about entering the medical world, but thankful that I'd concentrated in my anatomy lessons!

Again, I shouldn't have worried. This was such an amazing job! It was in a private practice in Manchester's equivalent of Harley Street for a high-profile sports physio. It was so busy, with 60 plus patients each day, many world-class sports stars and TV celebrities. I gained so much knowledge about anatomy, injuries and treatments.

It was fantastic training. I had to welcome and help treat four patients every half hour. It was a crash course in patient management and how to run a hugely successful clinic.

Two years later, I felt I should get back to my first love – beauty – and perhaps, work on the cruise ships (and maybe stop off in Hollywood to be a makeup artist!).

However, fate took another turn, we were so busy in the clinic I couldn't attend interviews for the cruise ships, so my career plan was again disrupted.

So, I took the opportunity to set up a beauty salon in a local health club. This was again, out of my comfort zone, as I hadn't worked in the beauty sector before, and here I was, running my own business. I should have trusted my intuition; it proved to be a great move.

One of my first clients wanted me to recreate a week's visit to a residential spa, so I planned a full week's programme which included fitness activities alongside lots of treatments. She loved it and repeated it a few months later !

This started my fascination with the wonderful benefits of spas and a lifelong quest to visit as many as possible around the world. (It's a dirty job, but someone's got to do it!)

Working within the health club was a great experience. I developed a wide range of treatments, especially body therapies, probably inspired by my time working in the physio practice. During this time, I also had a lot of celebrity clients. The physio practice referred clients to me, plus many artists working in ballet, theatre, TV and film sought out my so-called *magic hands*. I then opened a second salon in Manchester, juggling three roles, as I had also returned part-time to the physio clinic.

Around this time, some friends started to teach beauty therapy, and in a moment of madness, I wondered if it might be an option for me, too. But it scared me and I felt it was seriously out of my reach.

Whilst at College, a friend said she wanted a career *teaching* Beauty and I thought she was crazy. I can honestly say it was the furthest thing from my mind. Never in a million years did I ever consider teaching. It seemed so frightening because when I was growing up, I was very shy and didn't ever want to be the centre of attention. Teaching sounded horrific, with the focus on you, stood at the front of the class.

It was never in my plans. However, the universe had a different path mapped out, and I found myself applying for part-time teaching hours (Eeek!).

Guess what? I absolutely loved it! It was a very difficult start. I wasn't much older than my students and I had to work long hours to plan and prepare everything from scratch. In those days, before computers, I had to use a typewriter to prepare my handouts, with accompanying hand drawn diagrams (my drawing of a sheep to demonstrate lanolin was legendary!).

However, as hard it was, it was equally rewarding. I loved helping students develop excellent skills and high standards, so they became successful Therapists. My previous love of anatomy came to the fore and unlike many other tutors, I enjoyed teaching this subject - origins, insertions and actions of muscles were a particular favourite!

I always ensured students were aware of all the fabulous opportunities the sector had to offer and they got great work experience and had a chance to enter competitions. We also included guest speakers, masterclasses and trips to Paris.

I was blessed to have a great boss who gave her full backing to any new ideas I had, and together we built the department from one group of 12 students to over 1,000 learners.

At this time holistic and wellbeing courses were just starting to gain popularity and we maximised this opportunity. I developed full-time Holistic Therapy programmes, as well as a wide range of part-time options. We had multiple courses including aromatherapy, reflexology nutrition, counselling, Tai'Chi and Shiatsu.

It felt like we were ahead of our time, so much was on offer. Eve Taylor came to train our team in an exciting new treatment – Aromatherapy – long before it was included in the curriculum. We had a holistic summer school which was so popular that people took a week off work to attend all the sessions. We also ran an annual mind, body and spirit festival, with lots of well-being activities plus occasionally the Whirling Dervishes and a North American Shaman in a tepee on the college lawn! I loved the innovation and the fact that students were progressing to careers in spas and wellness clinics. They really were the glory days of adult education; colleges were packed with adults taking a huge range of courses. It makes me envious for the opportunities we had to respond to the needs of adults, improving their career prospects as well as enhancing their lives and overall wellbeing.

I look back on this period as the time I became more enlightened and spiritual, I started to trust and follow my instinct and intuition and I learnt to not worry about rigid plans, or going on detours, instead to simply allow things to flow. My pixie dust became legendary also and helped with many Ofsted visits!

I loved the management side at college and started to gain promotion to Team Leader, Head of Department, Director and then Assistant Principal. FE is an amazing sector, often undervalued, but so vitally important in the lives of many young people, adults and employers. It embraces everyone and enhances lives in a million different ways. I could write an entire book on my experience in FE over 25 years. It has given me opportunities I never imagined I would have and has developed me in hundreds of ways.

As a Beauty Therapy Educator you are a dual professional, you have the best (or worst) of both worlds, you have to keep up to date with all your skills and knowledge of the beauty industry, as well as keep up to date with your teaching skills and pedagogy. Although I was reluctant to try teaching, I now would certainly recommend it as a career, but it's definitely not for the faint- hearted. It takes a huge amount of hard work, patience, resilience and attention to detail to be a great teacher. I'd also put a huge emphasis on humour, it helps you enjoy the journey, especially if you can laugh at yourself.

With many years of experience, I've become less worried about falling. Instead, I try and focus on all the positives and how well it could go... *what if I fly?* I get involved in lots of different projects, many based around beauty and competitions such as WorldSkills UK activity.

Alongside my role in Further Education I have always kept close links with *Habia*, the government recognised standard setting body for the hair and beauty industry. I'm currently Chair of Habia, it's a privilege and a pleasure to be involved, they develop National Occupational Standards (NOS), champion high professional standards (both nationally and internationally) and work to serve and support the hair and beauty sector. I keep up to date with developments in the beauty and spa sector by visiting spas around the world, I write short reviews of my favourite spas and am often asked for recommendations. I've written a spa book which involved an amazing trip to 20 spas in Thailand, Dubai, India and Iceland.

I truly feel I've got a dream career, combining lots of my passions — beauty, spas, education, competitions and travel. I'm blessed that my beauty therapy qualification has given me so many opportunities, with lots more to come.

My path hasn't followed my original plan, but I wouldn't have it any other way (I'd have hated Hollywood!)

I urge you to embrace every opportunity, push outside your limits and allow yourself to find what's truly meant for you. Work hard and be kind, but don't forget to also believe in a little bit of magic. And keep your sense of humour at all times.

For any young person in a small village wondering what the world holds for them... it holds fantastic opportunities, amazing experiences and a chance to live the life you dream of... so, get ready to take off.

To soar.

* *With reference to Erin Hanson's poem, *What If I Fall?*

About Joan Scott

Joan is a Beauty and Spa expert, and an award-winning educationalist, specialising in apprenticeships and adult education and is currently Assistant Principal at Trafford College Group (TCG). Joan believes passionately that skill competitions help learners to accelerate their careers.  She is an Ambassador for the Association of Colleges (AoC) promoting WorldSkills UK and recently won the Times Education Supplement (TES) WorldSkills UK Hero Award.

Joan is the Chair of HABIA, the government recognised national standards body that promotes excellence and professionalism. She also hosts Education Forums to keep educators aware of current challenges and opportunities. Joan is author of *The Official Guide to Spa Therapy* and has contributed to many industry textbooks.

Her light-hearted website, *Beauty Hound,* shares new beauty products and treatments.

Contact Joan

Joan.scott@tcg.ac.uk

http://www.beautyhound.co.uk/joan-scott

*Instagram: @habiauk_ and @beautyhound_*

*Twitter: @Joanscott_ and @beautyhound_*

Life Is What You Make Of It
How My Darkest Times Pushed Me To Make The Most Important Decision Of My Life

Marta Zaczkowska

I wanted to be a lawyer. Not because I loved law and wanted to practise but because being a lawyer would give me a better and more comfortable life and some sort of prestige. After completing my first year, my family's circumstances dramatically changed. We lost our beloved grandmother. My dad couldn't bare this loss, stopped working and got into alcohol addiction.

I knew then life wasn't going to be easy.

I got a part time job at local tanning shop where one day someone had dropped off a leaflets from the local beauty college advertising beauty courses. I didn't pay much attention until one day after talking to my friends I started thinking about dropping out of law school and getting quick qualifications instead.

I hoped this would give me a ticket to freedom and help me escape the difficult relation with my dad.

I was far from being girly or fashionable, I never cared about makeup, though the only thing I always took care of were my nails.

My mum wasn't happy. I remember her saying, *"I would rather see you doing law than beauty treatments on someone's feet."*

My mum thought like many parents in Poland, you must have a degree and be a lawyer or doctor.

I promised myself that if I went to beauty college, I would be the best student there and finish with the best grades. I wanted my parents to be proud of me.

So that's what I did.

I love my country, don't get me wrong, but something in me was always pushing to explore and think outside the box. I knew I wasn't going to stay in Poland forever, so it was no surprise when I moved to London in 2006.

By then I was a qualified beauty therapist. I quickly found a job at a tanning shop in central London where they wanted me to do just waxing.

I had to face two challenges.

First, I didn't speak English. I had only studied German at school. And second, I wasn't experienced in waxing. But after ten months of practising everyday I found true passion and my ideal job. My English improved quickly and clients started asking for appointments with me. Life was good.

I only started to think about leaving the tanning shop after the work conditions and the management style became impossible to accept.

One day I left, and never went back. From that day I knew I never wanted to work for anyone else. I wanted to be my own boss. I just had to figure out how to make this happen.

Shortly after leaving I decided to first work from home. I started to advertise online for clients. It was 2007 and Facebook was only three years old. I wasn't busy straightaway. But over time and lots of effort it got better.

I started to get online reviews and my portfolio and reputation as a waxing specialist started to grow. I had clients from all over London.

During the five years of running my business from home I've learnt how to manage my time, money, stock, bookings and online advertising. And while I was self-employed I sensed that something was coming and was going to change my life forever.

It's 2011, and I was doing really well but I became pregnant. It was total shock and I wasn't prepared for it. My partner decided immediately that he wasn't going to be a part of it and I was soon alone without family and friends.

The future didn't look good. I had to make some decisions and it was a difficult one. The situation changed me on many levels. I cried and cried for a long time until I didn't have any tears left.

I woke up one day and thought, *Right I need to be more responsible, I need to protect my future and have a stable income. I am going to open a salon.*

It was like therapy for me. It took away the pain, disappointment and shame.

I started to visualise exactly what I wanted. I was practising the law of attraction. You see, I love the book *The Secret* by Rhonda Byrne; it has had a massive impact on me - on my beliefs, skills and actions. I didn't have the money or the knowledge on how to open a salon but I was so determined to that dream.

I needed help. I knew a highly successful business owner. He was happy to share knowledge and helped me create a business plan. The rest I had to do myself.

I believed I could create a single service business that focused entirely on waxing. I knew that once women tried my services they would come back.

I secured a loan with the bank and within five months I opened Waxing Specialist in Clapham, London. Wait, did I mention the salon was on the same road as my flat, just 10-minute walk? And the rent was exactly what I wrote down on my wish list? Crazy, right, but that is how the law of attraction works.

I remember being criticised about the name and the business model.

I called it Waxing Specialist to give a clear message to clients that I am indeed a specialist, I am good at it and I love it. So it made sense to me to call the salon this way and do the only service that I am passionate about.

Let me tell you, when I started there were only two high street salons in London offering just waxing and they were large established companies. I was just a girl with a dream and a small startup company.

Waxing Specialist was growing rapidly and very quickly I had to hire staff. And suddenly I became a brand with a reputation of being the best intimate waxing specialists in London. We started to offer intimate pregnancy and post pregnancy waxing. I also encouraged my staff to enter awards to showcase the set of skills they had learnt from me.

In 2014, I decided to replace the receptionist with a 24-hour online booking system integrated into the website. It was a brave yet risky move but I knew it would work. From then on you could only make appointments by booking online. Clients quickly learnt the new way.

I also introduced a strict cancellation policy and charges for missed appointments. The no-show losses decreased from £600 per month to £200, but this time was that we had the fees for no-shows in a bank account.

Owning a salon meant wearing so many hats and I had plenty of new challenges to face. I needed to invest in training and self-development. I also decided to hire a business mentor, which meant stepping out of the treatment room, entirely.

It took about two years to fill the gaps in my skills and knowledge about business.

Since then I have completed management courses, assertiveness skill courses, and leadership skills for women in business. I learned so much about myself by doing the Gallup Strength Finder test and discovered that my five top strengths are: focus, competition, learner, significance, and responsibility. Now I felt stronger than ever.

I systemised my business by creating blueprints and systems that brought the business to the point where I didn't have to be there for it to run smoothly.

But I wasn't finished yet.

As a highly focused person I felt like I needed a new challenge. I decided to qualify as a teacher and open Waxing Specialist Academy. I wanted to share my knowledge with others.

Looking at my life story you most likely realise that the tough times are the ones that sharpen my focus and get me to work harder.

During the pandemic and the first lockdown in 2020, I opened a consultancy business. I now offer a range of digital products which are designed to help other beauty professionals to become excellent waxing specialists.

It's great being a part of such an amazing industry. I also still feel that I have so much more to give. I am looking forward to the future.

I truly believe that taking opportunities, going with my gut feeling and consistent effort is the key to the success of my story.

Don't be afraid to go for what you want, and trust the process. Never give up. The universe will always be on your side.

About Marta Zaczkowska

Marta Zaczkowska is an International Waxing Expert and Consultant with over 16 years of experience specialising in intimate hair removal and pregnancy waxing. She is the owner of the highly respected Waxing Specialist Salon and Academy, located in Central London.

Marta's unwavering passion for the highest standards, coupled with industry demand for specialist help from fellow waxers, has resulted in her setting up Marta Zaczkowska Consultancy, where she advises salon owners on how to take their waxing practice to a whole new level of profitability, professionalism and expertise.

She has created several unique online resources including the *The Waxing Audit* designed to spotlight and improve techniques plus the first-ever accredited pregnancy intimate waxing course and female intimate waxing course called the *Intimate Wax Formula*.

Marta instinctively recognises the various challenges waxing business owners and prospective waxing specialists are facing, and has conducted multiple webinars and conference seminars to help. She is also a regular contributor for specialist trade and press articles.

Contact Marta

marta@waxingspecialist.co.uk

https://www.martazaczkowska.com/

https://www.facebook.com/groups/482681405963772

https://www.instagram.com/martazaczkowska_/

https://www.youtube.com/user/WAXINGSPECIALIST

I Grew My Business Organically

Sarah Hurst

My interest in the beauty industry started when I was 13.

My parents were entrepreneurs. My father, a pharmacist, had his own chemist shop in Ripley, Derbyshire. My mother worked alongside him as the company secretary. They expanded and added a photography department, a café, a video department and a beauty salon.

I went to boarding school. During the holidays, I helped in my parent's business and loved it. The beauty industry was quite new back in the late 1970s and although I couldn't observe treatments, I spoke with the therapist who worked there and developed a real interest in wanting to help and serve at a deeper level than over a counter. I wanted to make a real difference as to how people felt about themselves.

My teachers at school tried to talk me out of it and direct me towards other careers. I tried to keep an open mind, but my interest never waned.

After completing O-Levels, I started my Beauty Training under Dawn Cragg's team of tutors at the Park school of

Beauty Therapy in Retford, Nottinghamshire, undertaking a two-year course and gaining several highly recognised international qualifications. I loved it and qualified in 1988.

I relocated from Derbyshire to London after gaining a job as a therapist in a top London salon. I didn't work there for too long as my boss showed no support whatsoever and I couldn't develop. I became disillusioned and dropped out of the industry for a while.

I was 19. My level of training was high. I decided to set up on my own, doing mobile work. I approached a bank, armed with a business plan and cashflow forecast and secured a loan that was enough to set me up. After relocating to Surrey from London with my boyfriend, we had flyers printed and one weekend we delivered them. I also put an advert in the local paper. The phone started ringing and bookings were coming in. I was on my way.

After 18 months, my boyfriend's job was relocated to Brighton. My business was doing well, so I commuted three days a week to keep my clients going whilst I established myself in Brighton. This wasn't as quick and easy as in rural Surrey. My boyfriend and I split up after 18 months, but I liked Brighton so I decided to stay. I concentrated on continuing to build my mobile business which was gaining momentum.

I met someone else, married in 1994, and fell pregnant within a few months. I changed my business to set it up in my spare room and offer less mobile work.

By 1997, I was pregnant for the second time and needed more space. We moved house which gave me a larger treatment room plus the space we needed for our growing family.

The next few years were tough. Business was doing well, but my private life was a disaster. My husband was drinking. I also had a severe prolapsed disc in my low back and struggled to function. I gave up any residual mobile work so I didn't have to carry the equipment but couldn't give up work completely to recover as I had to support the family. My husband and I split up in 2002. My children were four and six. My back was operated on in 2003 and it gave me my life back! I had struggled to walk. The disc had caused severe scoliosis as well as sciatica. When I got out of bed after the operation the pain was mostly gone, and I was standing up straight. A miracle. I had taken mobility for granted. It was after this that I discovered my love of hiking.

I was in a new relationship with a man who was (and still is) incredibly supportive.

Fast forward to 2008. My children were becoming teenagers and they weren't very mindful of their volume levels. I loved, however, being there for the children and being able to work around them. I set up a studio in my garden that housed two treatment rooms. I loved having my own, separate working space.

Throughout my whole career I continued to develop myself. The beauty industry is fast paced and I strived to be one of the best, with a high level of knowledge and up to date treatments. I wanted to pass on that knowledge to others and therefore I decided to look into teaching in further education.

When you complete your Certificate in Education you teach alongside it. I secured a part-time position teaching, in the main, electrolysis to the Level 3 students.

I was about to start university and teaching when life threw me a major curve ball. My sister had Grade 3 breast cancer. I was devastated. The prognosis wasn't positive. I pursued my goals, but mentally it was a challenging period of my life. My sister fought hard, but the disease got the better of her. She passed away in February 2010, just months before I completed my teacher training.

I loved teaching, but I was exhausted. My business was still growing in leaps and bounds and after everything I had been through I decided to make some massive life changes. I left teaching in the summer of 2011 and employed my first therapist to help me out in my home Studio. Sophie was straight out of college but willing to learn and turned into a fantastic therapist who stayed for three years.

After years of working by myself, it was a big change to employ someone else, but it was another way to teach and pass things forward.

One day in October 2014, I saw that a local salon had closed. I had considered my own salon several times, but it had never felt the right time. My kids were much older now, so this seemed like my opportunity. However, I didn't have the funds. Then, one of my clients who I'd known for a long time, offered to loan me the money! I know plenty of people who would advise against this arrangement, but for us it has worked perfectly. I completely refitted the salon and we opened in March 2015.

Sophie moved on and I took on a new team of three.

My business had always specialised in electrolysis and we were well known for this. We were performing most of the commonly found beauty treatments and started to build up a keen following for skin treatments.

I trained in Accor Plasma Pen which I love, which led to an opportunity to be a national trainer. I also helped the Smart Group develop their protocols for their new SmartMeso treatment.

In 2019, we decided to rebrand as a skin clinic, offering non invasive skin treatments as well as hair removal. We dropped our nail treatments, spray tanning and ear piercing because we didn't enjoy them and they weren't profitable. Rebranding was a bigger job than I originally anticipated as it's not just about the change of signage or logo, it's about changing our complete message and promoting who we are.

By the beginning of 2020 we felt that we were ready to move forward with our message. We started to hear about a new virus that became increasingly worrying and by March we were closed. This was devastating for the whole country and set me towards fresh challenges. I really felt burnt out by the time we hit lockdown with all the stress.

I used this time to work on learning and my own mindset. Mindset is a new journey that I will now continue for the rest of my life.

- Keep learning and developing yourself and your team.
  It is so important that you keep up to date with your knowledge. This will also help you become experts in your field and possibly specialise in a particular area.

- Achieve a work/life balance. It is so important to look after yourself and not to reach burnout otherwise you are no good to anyone, particularly yourself. Do exercise, have hobbies, spend time with family. Whatever makes you tick and happy.

- Get yourself a mentor. I went many years trying to do everything on my own and impeded my own growth. I have learnt so much from other people.

- Don't be afraid to make mistakes. This will be the source of your biggest learning. However do try and avoid *Shiny Object Syndrome* and cherry pick.

I am so excited to see what the future brings both personally and professionally. I am starting a three year Naturopathic Nutrition Diploma and I have been approached by one of the major wholesalers about being an expert in their magazine. Whilst I write this we are closed again due to the pandemic lockdown (2021), which brings its own set of challenges, but over the last few months I have been starting to move towards establishing an online side, with an online shop and online consultations.

My aim is to work hard to regain confidence once we can fully reopen, and to continue with my love of training.

About Sarah Hurst

Sarah Hurst is a Beauty Therapist and is the founder of Sarah Hurst Skin Clinic, which is based in Brighton. Having been in the industry for 32 years, Sarah's experience is vast and has also been a teacher in Further Education. She has qualifications such as CIDESCO, CIBTAC and ITEC along with DTTLS (Diploma in Teaching in the Lifelong Learning Sector). However, she believes that learning is a lifelong journey.

Sarah's clinic specialises in non-invasive skin treatments promoting treating the skin from the inside out, by balancing gut health as well as how the skin is treated with homecare and in clinic treatments. This addresses the full solution to achieving flawless skin naturally. All forms of hair removal are also a speciality, such as Electrolysis, Laser and Waxing.

Sarah is also a trainer for the *Smart Group* and has assisted with developing treatments and you will also find her assisting them at the major beauty exhibitions.

Sarah is really passionate about personal and business development. She has two grown up children.

Contact Sarah

https://sarahhurstskinclinic.co.uk

https://facebook.com/sarahhurstskinclinic

https://instagram.com/sarahhurstskinclinic

https://www.linkedin.com/in/sarah-hurst-9825207/

Real Dreams Are Worth Fighting For

Jill Yvette Painter

My school days were a little different. They meant big homemade daily micropore and lint bandages, concealed beneath my clothes, covering painful eczema. No child wants to be labelled *special* at school, but in my case, special treatment was needed, along with visits to the GP.

A defining moment came in 1976 at 14 years old, when I awoke with serious eczema on my face. This time the amazing male GP recommended using Delph skin care products and a prescription for the biggest tube of Dermovate (strongest steroid) to use sparingly!

In 1979, I sat in front of the career advisor at sixth form who asked, *What's an Aesthetician? Wouldn't you prefer an office?*

Forgive me, but I am reasonably bright, and more suited to a creative practical job. Office work is not my dream! I promptly walked out, and arranged a day experience in a beauty salon myself. The nearest beauty college/training was miles away with limited options. I applied, but was rejected due to my eczema.

This painful condition has created a stubborn streak in me: a passion, drive and survival instinct. I met Dawn Cragg an inspiring and forward thinking lady, at the Park School of Beauty, in Retford, Nottinghamshire. The school offered specialist makeup training, aromatherapy and reflexology as well as beauty therapy and electrolysis. My wonderful supportive parents (Dad a University lecturer, and Mum a Higher Ed teacher) found the funds to enable my dream to begin. Whilst there I won the ITEC fantasy makeup competition, and passed with Honours in 1981.

My first job was with Steiner in Leeds who supplied therapists to cruise ships. However, after working there and hearing stories, I vowed the only way I would cruise was as a passenger. TV's cruise star, Jane McDonald, I am not! Four months later, at 19 years old, I landed a peach job in my home town of Huddersfield, working for a new cosmetic distributor, Lady Esther. I got the job because of my makeup skills and all round training. Still only 19, I was trusted to run their beauty salon single handed - treating clients, writing and delivering in-house training courses and following reps around the country. We ran nationwide makeup competitions for college stockists of which I was a judge! (Thank you Dawn Cragg).

We did all the exhibitions and I even got filmed by the local TV station while applying mascara, and fantasy makeup for an audience of 1000 for a stockist. It was all exciting and very special, giving me great insight and experience and lots of chances to wear designer evening dresses!

At 22, I bought the salon from Lady Esther and began my next dream for a chain of Jill Yvette's Holistic Beauty's. The classy salon expanded to six staff and a satellite salon.

Business was thriving. My eczema and allergies had been reasonably dormant up to now, except for discovering a sensitivity to wheat and dairy (which was confirmed by my GP). However, later I had a time in hospital when I realised the NHS institution did not yet fully recognise any allergies or their treatment. This created my interest and personal drive for information and knowledge in diets and holistic therapies for self-help.

My health problems are both a curse and an advantage, depending on your viewpoint. I decided I was never going to be a victim. They are a part of who I am and make me a stronger fighter. The unique real-life knowledge will drive and work for me. Experience of hospitals and allergy clinics gives me a deep and unique sympathy with clients who are struggling. My holistic perspective enables me to 'join the dots' - and think out of the box, finding the cause within. I could never be a machine led therapist. It is not pure enough for my own body!

I Believe In Fate Especially Since Reiki Found Me

I believe beauty, wellbeing, listening and helping one to one with client problems is my way of following in my Dad's heritage of Methodist preachers. My Dad played a big part in my life professionally and personally. He was my guide, friend and mentor, and proudest believer in me. We shared many ideas, methods, chats. Reiki helps me share those skills. After eight years at Reiki Second Degree level, I achieved my Reiki Master/Teacher qualification.

I was teaching my first course to friends when I found out my Dad had cancer. Our world fell apart - but we tried to keep strong for each other. During that last six months, we bonded more than ever during daily Reiki sending sessions. I was able to ease his suffering and finally able to give back to him. It gave us both comfort. The Yorkshireman finally got a return on his initial investment all those years ago. Losing him was my biggest loss ever. If you ever find a true mentor, listen and give respect and thanks.

Four weeks after losing Dad, a new client with terminal cancer came to me asking for Reiki. I declined, explaining about my dad. Her reply, *That's exactly why I now know, you are the best person to help me!*

Her trust is a powerful and positive memory for me.

Reiki is my belief system. I feel it looks out for me, shows me the way. If things are tough, I ask Reiki, *What lesson do I have to learn to move forward?*

Reality Check

The salon business empire was not the dream I had expected. The management side took me away from my clients. After three years of business I realised I had enjoyed the prestige but preferred to help clients directly. I had lots to offer; holistic improvements come from within themselves if they know how, not just a miracle jar of cream. It is rewarding and wonderful to see a client's health, confidence and happiness grow.

A One Woman Success Story

Throughout my career, I have won or been a finalist for awards:

- Gernetician of the year

- Customer Care

- Beauty Therapist of the Year

Proving age and experience is beneficial, my proudest award was in 2012, at the age of 50:

- BABTAC - 'British Beauty Industry Entrepreneur of the Year' for creating I wish...® The Wellbeing Facial Therapy

That last one is for you Dad!

I Wish...®

I wish...® is my signature therapy, taking 30 years to develop based on experience and feedback from clients. Using specialist products - especially Monsieur Laporte's 'Gernetic' products, plus holistic therapies, wellbeing knowledge, and my special 'X' factor. I created new unique techniques and methods for the whole therapy.

I wish...® is an intuitive two hours of bespoke luxury - a unique powerful therapy. It is *still* before its time; no two treatments are the same. Clients ride a wave of emotions, and experiences as they finally allow themselves to let go and heal themselves mentally, physically and emotionally.

I wish...® can create miracles, is breathtaking and more powerful than any other therapy I know.

In 2010, clients had encouraged me to teach *I wish...*® to therapists. With the aid of a government research grant, I began my biggest, costliest two-year project. Research, thrice-weekly lectures via Business Link, teaching qualification, accreditations, trademarks, designing, websites, social media etc. regularly stepping right out of my comfort zone. And all whilst running a fully booked salon with waiting list for new clients - alone! It was hard, but enjoyable. I could not have done it without support from my very patient husband.

Tips From Research Lectures

Here is a list of thoughts to steer by, that have helped me, if you have ideas you believe in:

- Preparation is essential; never 'wing it'

- Working alone the more knowledgeable and flexible you are - gaining more skills - the better. In business you may need many hats

- Teaching courses need to be practical, fun and enjoyable

- Don't 'erm' whilst talking, and be decisive with business decisions

- Think out of the box

- Employ others to do specialised tasks - it's more cost effective using your time to treat clients

- The best advice is freely offered

- Acknowledge something is not working before costs explode, take a 'Dragons Den' viewpoint

- The beauty and health business will always fit around
  your circumstances - no two therapists are the same.

- When starting a business - research thoroughly. There are more
  rules and regulations than ever before e.g. GDPR, current health
  and safety, etc. and not for the faint hearted.

- Believe and be brave.

- Understand your personality and what makes you work better.
  For me I am an Obsessive perfectionist, so projects create focus,
  and deadlines suit me. Otherwise I would never stop!

- Remember Perfection never comes. Finish, finalise and plan
  as much as possible, but remember at some point of reality
  plan 'B' will present itself. Be prepared to use it.

The Present - My Legacy

When my 85 year old mum fell and broke her hip, I became her carer. I reduced my hours to part-time, and set up *The Annex* in three rooms of my home. I think of myself as a genuine professional with a big heart, a business-minded therapist with knowledge and experience second to none, who happens to work from home. Regardless, I still create top-notch unequalled therapies.

Remember, as long as there is stress, wellbeing, health problems, and beauty tweaks to do, Holistic Beauty will always be needed.

My legacy is making a real difference in this world. Current pandemic restrictions make the human *survival psyche* kick in and find alternative ways through new beginnings, re-assessing priorities, and even *Dreams of a new you* and new struggles to achieve that. Ten months on from the pandemic's emergence, those alternatives are being observed worldwide. We can emerge in a stronger position, and evaluate life for tomorrow and the future..

So what is your dream?

So, What Is Your Dream?

Having a dream creates drive. If you do not have *dreams,* what pleases you in life? Try out ideas. Create a visual picture board with four sections:

- Your Likes

- Your Hopes

- What's Important

- Purpose of your life, your legacy

Then sit and quietly, reflect. Use the visual board for inspiration and for discovering your dreams.

And do not forget to think out of the box!

About Jill Yvette Painter

Jill Yvette's ambition since 14 years old was to work in the beauty profession. She is a well-experienced and respected holistic Beauty Therapist with 40 years in the trade, and whose experience has covered most aspects of it.

Fighting through her own health problems has enabled her to be inspired through her own experiences to delve deeply into holistic natural methods. This story explains those fights, and helping clients too with her unique knowledge and application, leading to winning awards.

She is married and proud to live in Huddersfield, in God's own County of Yorkshire. Where it is stunning, green and lumpy.

Contact Jill

info@jillyvettes.co.uk

https://www.jillyvettes.co.uk

https://www.facebook.com/JillYvettesHolisticBeauty

TripAdvisor https://bit.ly/3inUmFF

GLOW Is Teamwork

Sara Shoemark

I adore our industry, however, as a teen it was not my life-long dream to be part of this amazing profession. I spent my teenage years an odd shade of orange, wore far too much makeup and did not really know what I wanted to do with my life. My mum was, and still is amazing, never judging my youthful disasters and just supporting, sorting and always celebrating my achievements.

Looking back, I loved to please, to make those around me happy, and I suppose, like us all, I love to be loved.

After a few trial careers failed to inspire, I began my journey in the late 1980s, training at The Ray Cochrane Beauty School, London. And wow! I fell head-over-heels in love with this wonderful industry. Maybe unappreciated then, but I was blessed to have a scary yet totally inspirational and beautiful Principle, Miss Suri. She sent me home more than once for not wearing a petticoat and for this level of discipline I am forever grateful. I can assure you I needed it and to this day I hold her values close to all that I do in my life.

I was fortunate to then work in a number of prestigious

spas and stores, involving both retail and beauty therapy, to include *Harrods, Selfridges* and *Fortnum and Mason.*

After gaining valuable experience and a wealth of knowledge I moved home to the north in 1990 and completed a teacher training course alongside teaching beauty therapy at a college in Cheshire.

Whilst teaching was both enjoyable and worthwhile, I missed hands-on treatments and the joy and interaction of helping clients to look and feel their best. However, in these early days of the high street beauty salon, I could not find a professional salon within which to work. There was not one within at least a two-hour commute - how times have changed. This was instrumental in my decision to start my own treatment room and 'Beauty with Sara' was born!

I opened in one room, above a hair salon, and from my first client until today I refused to compromise. Implementing all that I had experienced and learnt into all that I did, ensuring the client received only the best, most advanced treatment with the highest quality of products in a small but professional, hygienic and beautiful surrounding, thereby giving every single customer the best experience possible. Clients fell in love with their treatments and word spread fast. At the time I was fortunate, they had no choice, there was no competition. Now I must work harder. Our industry has grown beyond belief, this is wonderful and it is now up to me to ensure they have an experience so amazing that the customer has no choice but to return to GLOW.

As the popularity of the salon grew, I had to twice move to bigger premises. This growth continued and has culminated today in our GLOW group of salons based in Wrexham,

Chester and Mold. Maybe I would have grown further but I was blessed that my husband and I sneaked three children into our equation, they are now 18, 19 and 21. They are beyond amazing and alongside my husband, are my whole world.

But maybe it is now time to grow GLOW a little more.

I now love to support and watch our wonderful therapists grow, giving them the confidence to believe in themselves. I am grateful for the time they spend with GLOW and I work with them to discover their strengths and passions, develop their skills and achieve what they wish to achieve. I learn from them too and surround myself with a diverse team, of varied strengths and skills who have a far greater knowledge of their speciality than myself. I simply support and guide them. All I ask of them is while they are with us is that they commit to GLOW and work to the beliefs and standards we all must constantly and consistently aspire to. If they chose to move in a different direction I support this too and will help them follow their own dreams whatever these may be. I am humbled that a large number of our lovely local salons began their journey alongside me and still get in touch for support and advice.

I am passionate, enthusiastic, can be brave, annoyingly optimistic, and prepared to work incredibly hard, but as we grew, I knew, if I wanted to secure future success there are times when it is essential to seek specialist support. Their contribution was an essential part of the continual development of our salons. We further achieved success with a change of brand identity, from 'Beauty with Sara' to 'GLOW'. It was a market-led decision and one I felt necessary in our fast-moving industry.

I will always outsource things in areas that I know nothing or little about and I focus my energy on my strengths and ensuring that GLOW continually moves forward, embracing the future alongside always instilling our basic values.

Before college courses were more available, we became a City and Guilds accredited training centre. A necessity to grow and develop to the standards that were essential to me. I began to train my own therapists, along with providing training for other salons after a number of our own therapists achieved their assessor qualifications. Although we still train every day ensuring we are constantly moving forward, at present we are not affiliated with a professional, verified body so must outsource to qualify and certificate. This is something my team and I wish to strive towards again, to work alongside a verified professional body, offering basic and advanced training to our own and other future therapists, giving our teams more diverse and exciting opportunities within GLOW whilst helping ensure we commit to raising standards and values of our future therapists.

My belief has always been to provide an exceptional service, expertly executed. Results driven, personalised treatments with the essential and continuous necessity of the highest of quality verified training, with the best products, in a safe and beautiful environment, allowing clients to escape the stresses of life, promote an inner calm and thus a beauty that brings happiness and positively glows.

To date, GLOW have amassed shelves full of glittering national beauty awards for our Salons, UK Salon, Customer Care and Retailing. Individual therapists have pushed themselves beyond all they believed possible and achieved Therapist, Facialist and Manicurist awards and personally

I was humbled to be awarded, for three consecutive years, *Salon Director of the Year* at the *British Beauty Awards*. I have a sincere understanding that winning an award does not mean you are the best but by entering such a stringent process, I learn so much and always improve. To receive the respect of fellow professionals is awesome and I was totally honoured when *Professional Beauty* readers, more than once, voted GLOW as *UK's Most Inspiring Salon*. This year I was named as one of *Professional Beauty's Top 100 Industry Influencers*. I was overawed.

The process of entering awards, the nominations received and the awards, when won, also help to secure our future in this fast moving, incredible industry, opening doors for us all. But, maybe, the greatest reward is the pride of our clients and the smiles of our incredible team.

From work experience students to apprentices, therapists, fellow salon owners, journalists, entrepreneurs, marketing and business specialists and consultants, I have met so many incredible, beautiful and inspirational people. They have all taught me so much. I love to give something back too and if I can, I will.

A five minute call can sometimes help someone more than we could ever know. On a professional level, when my time allows, I offer select consultancy work for new or under achieving salons. I am always amazed at the benefits that can be given from just one single, short salon visit. Often people have all that it takes to succeed, they just need direction, focus, some positivity and reassurance to move forward. It can be very lonely as a Salon Owner.

Every new experience teaches me so much.

In the late 1990s, I was approached by *Tesco* and enjoyed working and advising them on a small budget range of body products which were available in 400 *Tesco* stores nationwide. I involved my team too and they loved seeing their salon name on bottles of product in their local supermarket.

I regularly attend conferences, always learning and when invited to contribute or speak, I do - it is a privilege. I also love working with local schools and colleges. I feel fortunate when called upon to contribute to magazines and the media on beauty related topics and am honoured and delighted to have assisted with the judging process at national beauty awards for many years. I feel incredibly honoured to have recently joined the *BABTAC Board* and also work advising professional bodies such as *HABIA* and *VTCT*. All this gives me the opportunity to meet new people, learn new things and give a little back to an industry that has given me so much.

I never want to stop learning and feel blessed to meet so many inspiring people who continue to teach me so much. I do not wish to stand still and feel incredibly lucky to work in an industry I adore. I work closely alongside my team and fellow professionals with continuous passion, knowledge and total dedication to promote our beauty industry in as many areas as I can, in the positive, professional light it truly deserves.

To me our future GLOWs.

About Sara Shoemark

Sara Shoemark is the founder and owner of the multi-award winning GLOW Beauty. GLOW has been recognised by industry peers as an outstanding salon winning numerous National awards to include UK Salon, Customer Care and Therapists. Sara was awarded Salon Director of the Year for three consecutive years, and *Professional Beauty* readers voted GLOW, more than once, *UK's Most Inspiring Salon*. This year Sara was named as one of *Professional Beauty's Top 100 Industry Influencers*.

Sara speaks at colleges and is a regular presenter at conferences and as a judge at Professional Awards. She has previously worked with Tesco advising on a range of products available in 400 Nationwide stores and is regularly called on as a subject expert in the media.

Most recently, she has began working advising government qualification bodies and was inducted as a BABTAC Board member. Sara feels fortunate to work in an industry she adores and working alongside others with passion, knowledge and dedication, to promote professionalism and excellence in the beauty industry.

Contact Sara

sjshoemark@me.com

https://glow-beauty.com

The Road To Self-Satisfaction

Clare Reed

A short while ago I was contacted by an old school friend, his daughter wanted to start a career in beauty therapy and he had *conceded* this was her passion, could I help. At first I was flattered but this soon turned to frustration and disappointment that our industry is still thought of in that way!

I came from a predominately academic family but knew I was not that way inclined. School didn't interest me and university or an academic path was not on my radar, which was just as well as I left with virtually no qualifications, so my options were limited. I settled for a YTS scheme in the travel and tourism industry but it didn't excite me and frankly I wasn't very good at it. My feelings and skills were clearly noticed, as after the first year I was sacked!

With support from my parents I decided to start again and thought a Beauty Therapy course at my local college would be interesting and fun.

A little bit older, more mature and now realising an education was important, I knew I had to stick in.

To my surprise, I discovered I actually enjoyed learning, and worked hard. Now I had the opportunity to take another route. I was doing something to stimulate me and knew I was on the right path. I passed with flying colours and my parents couldn't have been more proud. I started work immediately in a local salon where I had previously done work experience and couldn't have been happier.

However this was short lived, as a year later, the owner decided to sell up. The beauty industry wasn't as prevalent as it is today, so there wasn't as many jobs available. I was deflated but knew there was a good therapist inside me and I wasn't going to let it go to waste.

A few months later, I got my break and started working for a large chain of salons within one of Newcastle's top department stores.

I spent 13 happy years there and gained invaluable experience, qualifications, high standards and confidence. I met some great influential people and I think it moulded me into the beauty therapist I am today. The job security enabled me to get on the property ladder and soon after, I got married.

After my second child was born, the long, inflexible hours no longer suited my family, I realised it was time for a change. I set up at home working from my converted garage and started to build up my business and to my delight some customers followed me from my previous position. I worked around my children and my husband's job.

My marriage broke down a few years later so we had to move, my new work space wasn't ideal and I knew it wouldn't provide enough financially stability now I that was paying the bills on my own. I was reluctant to leave behind the career I so loved, so I did my teaching qualifications and started delivering evening classes for my local council. I was passionate about sharing my knowledge with others and the students were great. It was tough working evenings as I had to arrange childcare but I stuck in and progressed to delivering daytime courses in a wide range of subjects to potential therapists and young women often from challenging and vulnerable backgrounds. Life was busy and sometimes tough, juggling running a home on my own, teaching, marking and still carrying out treatments in my spare time, it certainly was demanding. I sometimes found myself thinking *Is this it?* I was passing on my knowledge but missing more hands on beauty therapy.

Early on in a new term, some years later, I was asked to speak to a potential student. She had a salon ready to open, her skills were more business-based but her partner (the therapist) had let her down. She was now looking to do some fast track courses to enable her to open her salon. During this conversation my mind started going into overdrive... *Could I be this therapist? Could I have a salon?*

The idea excited me and sparked something in me that I hadn't felt in a long time. After all, isn't this what all therapists aspire to have one day? After much deliberation, and a loan from my ever supportive parents, to buy into the business, I decided to embark on a new journey of owning my own salon. I had reached my goal.

Like a lot of things in life, the road is not always smooth. As it transpired, this one was set to be an unmarked, pot-holed one and unfit for traffic!

Things started well. The plan was that my business partner would look after the day-to-day running of the salon and I would concentrate on what I loved and knew best, carrying out treatments. The plan was for her to take courses to enable her to carry out proposed future treatments once the salon had grown.

However, a few months into the partnership the cracks began to appear. I found myself increasingly running the salon on top of doing all the treatments on my own.

It became clear that my partner wasn't the business woman I had been led to believe. We disagreed on a lot of things and I reached a tipping point in the partnership. I hit a low and couldn't carry on working like that. I turned to some good friends for support and advice, and one even offered to lend me the money to buy my partner out. Unfortunately, my partner wanted to stay in the salon so I felt trapped!

On a cold February morning, I arrived at the salon to find most of my equipment sitting on the pavement. Our short-lived business partnership was over. So with my salon in the boot of my car I drove away feeling gutted, foolish and most of all, guilty for the money my parents had leant me.

Then followed months of legal battles and a favourable county court judgement. I was back to square one, but by then, I had lost my passion and had no spark or energy to start again. I felt my journey as a beauty therapist had come to an end!

However, my friends were having none of that, and through their love and support they helped me find a room to rent in a clinic, and so, I started again!

I was now very happy and surrounded by a lot of positive people. The business grew and expanded but after a few years I realised that I'd taken this business as far as I could. I needed more and felt I had more to offer.

Sometime later, I attended the funeral of a friend's father-in-law (I nearly didn't go as I didn't want to let clients down and cancel) but felt it was the right and respectful thing to do. There, I got chatting to a friend of the family. He was fun, interesting, and had such a positive outlook on life...

I married this man 18 months later!

Before the wedding as most couples do, we discussed our goals, plans and aspirations for our new life together. We agreed it was time for me to move on from my current work place and find new premises. Little did I know this would be sooner than we thought. A friend of my husband's attending our evening reception told me that a local, established salon in a fantastic location was on the market. Our honeymoon was spent viewing the historical sights of Rome and discussing the potential of our new business venture.

Two months later the salon was ours! And this time I used my own savings to buy it.

I'm still here. It's a small salon but very busy and I have so many plans for its future. There have been some bumpy times and the road has certainly had some twists and turns, but I'm content and feel like I have eventually reached my personal goal. I believe when you have a profession that you are passionate about, there is a drive inside you that keeps you going and for that I am very fortunate and grateful.

My message to that old school friend dealing with the *disappointment* of his daughter wanting to be a beauty therapist? Be proud that she has found a career she is passionate about, it could lead her down so many different paths with great opportunities, no matter which one she chooses.

I hope this advice inspires you, too!

About Clare Reed

Clare Reed is a successful salon owner, wife, mother of two and step mum of three. She lives In Newcastle upon Tyne in the north east of England.

She qualified in Beauty therapy 30 years ago and has worked in the industry ever since. During this time she has trained with some of the top brands including, Guinot, Decleor, Clarins, Caci, Jessica, Delilah and many more.

In the course of her career she obtained a teaching diploma in adult learning and has delivered a variety of Beauty courses in both colleges and the community across the north east.

Clare has also diversified into creating and selling beauty based gifts

Outside of work Clare volunteers for the charity Fareshare and enjoys her new found love of motor-homing.

Contact Clare Reed

complexionsbeauty13@gmail.com

https://www.complexionsbeauty.co.uk

https://www.facebook.com/complexionsbeautygosforth

https://www.instagram.com/complexions_beauty

Determination Is Definitely The Key To Success!

Susan Over

Little did I know back then that the military-style upbringing that I had was going to hold me in such good stead for my future career.

My father had been in the Parachute Regiment, and boy, didn't we all know it! I was one of four children. He would wake us up at the crack of dawn, throw open the curtains, declaring to us all that we were missing the best part of the day... no wonder I'm still always up now between 5.30 and 6am every morning.

He was a meticulous man, slightly edging on OCD at times, as everything definitely had its place.

To give you an example, not only did he paint the outside of his manhole cover but underneath it too ! You get my drift on how particular he was. That was my father to a T!

Now I try to achieve that level of perfection in everything I do. I don't always succeed, but I try. In this industry, the *that will do* attitude won't get you very far.

When I was born I was 11lbs and I seemed to grow in proportion to that. As a child my name at school was 'Fatty' and kids used to say, *Can you stand in goal, as you fill half of it?* You know that child who was always the last one to be picked for the team...? Well, that was me! Strangely it never seemed to get to me... or did it?

It was obvious to me even then that a lot of people judged you on how you looked and quite simply that would alter how you would begin to feel. This made me determined to work in an industry that helped people look and feel good both inside and out. I was now on a mission.

Armed with the appropriate qualifications I went off to college for two years and achieved everything I set out to do. Having passed my world prestigious CIDESCO exam I was ready to conquer the world.

This was over 35 years ago and at that time beauty salons were a very rare sight. I remember there being only two other salons in my area and as neither of them had any vacancies I decided to go down the hard route and start up by myself.

By this time my father had his own business so I knew that it was going to be hard work, working long hours and with the utmost dedication. Dad told me that he would set up a salon for me but the last thing I wanted was for everyone to say, *Your Daddy bought the salon for you...* I wanted to do it myself.

I was furiously independent and looking back, as stubborn as a mule. I don't know what I was thinking as I hadn't got a penny to my name, only just pure enthusiasm and determination.

One day while trying to bring me back to size, my father then said, *OK, you think you're so clever, carry on... you'll never make a go of it!*

That was the best thing he could have said to me as it was like a red rag to a bull. I was now more determined than ever to prove him wrong.

Immediately, I made an appointment to see my bank manager with only an imaginative plan in my head, together with all the youthful ideas under the sun.

Wow! It seems laughable, as nowadays that would never be allowed to happen. But he challenged me and at first he said, *No.* I was so disappointed and headed towards the door but immediately, he asked me to sit back down, declaring he was just testing me to see what I was made of.

I obviously passed the test as he lent me some appropriate money and told me that the only condition was that I had to double my borrowings by a certain amount of time.

And that's exactly what I did !

I began by renting a room above a hairdressers in town but, after a while, I knew that I wanted to expand, employ therapists and have my own name above the salon door, and that's just what I achieved.

I found a property just on the outskirts of town, on the ground floor with plenty of parking right outside. It was perfect. Clients that wanted to pop in and out with no makeup on or with a pink upper lip after waxing could dash straight in to their cars without bumping in to anyone. The ease and convenience for the clients, together with no parking charges was a definite winner.

Choosing a name for the salon was the fun part. I decided that I wanted something with my name in it. Having the name Susan Over offered several fabulous possibilities. The first name I thought of was *Head Over Heels* but I later decided that *All Over Beauty* was much better. As 'A' would be at the front of the directory! I hoped that clients would come across my business first and with 'Beauty' in the name it would make it self-explanatory.

I started working 8am-8pm Monday to Friday and 8am-4pm on Saturdays. I was so determined to succeed Within the first year I had great success and employed three therapists, one at a time.

I always wanted to expand into next door, but it wasn't available, so I came up with another plan. I decided to buy a van and had it kitted out with my salon name emblazened down the side. Therefore, I could offer a mobile service from the salon, too.

It was a success, but to a point. I soon worked out that I could carry out far more treatments in the salon in a certain timeframe than I could going mobile.

It was actually my bank manager that suggested that I should get another salon. My intention was to get a bigger salon and shut the original one down, but, I ended up keeping both.

Five years later, I expanded again. The premises next door became available so I knocked a hole through the wall! It was everything I'd ever dreamt of.

At one stage, I had over 25 employees in my team and both salons thrived beautifully until the recession hit in 2008.

This made me review all of my expenditures.

Times had changed. My husband and I had divorced and I had two young children to bring up by myself. My mother and mother-in-law had both died so I didn't have any family help to call on. To make matters worse, there were now so many beauty salons and mobile therapists popping up everywhere and many of my staff were on maternity leave. It was time to make a big decision...

It was a tough one, but I decided to close the second salon.

Having already expanded my original salon, it was the obvious choice. It was the most established and a larger property and it had more treatment rooms. The layout was better and it had its very own private car park. Luckily, after altering the rotas slightly, I was still able to keep all my therapists.

So you see, out of something bad, came something good. And would you believe the salon was bringing in the same amount of money as the two combined, with only the cost of one property and far fewer receptionists. Lesson learnt... big isn't always beautiful!

I'm so glad I made that choice as it has allowed me to invest a considerable amount of money into state of the art high tech equipment. I firmly believe it was my determination that got me through the tough times and my salon is now busier than ever. I will add that I have absolutely no intention on expanding ever again! I've got such amazing team to whom I'm truly grateful.

So, what did I learn along the way?

Well, when first starting out most therapists just travel round to gather everyone else's price lists and undercut them. This is a huge mistake. For starters, everyone has different overheads.

Try this. Work our *your* prices. Then add the VAT to those prices. Even if, at first, you're not VAT registered, charge VAT prices. Use the added money to grow your business. Once you become VAT registered it's very difficult to suddenly put your prices up by 20%, so do it from the very beginning. More so if you salon aims to exceed the VAT threshold in revenues.

If you have a good team and you want to keep them, be as flexible as possible. Job sharing is an excellent idea for most. Find out what's best for them, especially if they have a family. Find out what incentivises them. You'll be surprised... it's *not* always money. Time off or a treat is often higher on their priority list than anything else.

If you're looking for premises, think about the parking. It's really important. Convenience is a high priority for most of your clients.

Try to open late at least one or two evenings a week. Increasingly, a larger number of your clients will work and will want to keep their weekends free. Trial starting later... but finishing later.

Try not to discount. It is far better to add value. Whether it's a treatment or a product, it's great to add a little something that they haven't had before.

Document everything! Confirming all details, that you've agreed verbally with a follow-up email works.

Getting all clients' medical details and any allergies is essential, but observe your GDPR obligations, of course.

Documenting all the information about their treatments with dates - and any reactions - will be required by your insurance company.

Always issue a Contract of Employment to each member of staff stipulating any restrictions and full details of their employment.

Surround yourself with likeminded people and employ people that have the same values as you. I cannot emphasise this point enough.

But most important, have fun. It's a fabulous career to be in, making people look and feel better...

Enjoy it !

About Susan Over

Susan Over is a highly qualified Beauty Therapist and an Award Winning Salon Owner. She is very pro-active with a keen emphasis towards continuous, professional development. Her well established salon, *All Over Beauty*, is located in the picturesque market town of Bury St Edmunds, in Suffolk.

After working as a therapist in the salon for over three decades, Susan now uses her strong organisational skills to manage and promote the salon and to motivate the rest of her hardworking team.

Having worked closely with her local College of Further Education, Susan also tries to inspire budding students by presenting an annual *All Over Beauty Award* to the most hardworking top achiever.

Susan's philosophy in life has always been to *Work Hard and Play Hard* and with her great sense of humour and the wonderful people in her life, that's what she plans to continue to do.

Contact Susan

email@alloverbeauty.com

https://www.alloverbeauty.com/#

https://en-gb.facebook.com/ALLOVERBeauty1

https://www.instagram.com/alloverbeautybse

The Mountains Of Life And Business

Maria Mason

I have climbed many mountains physically in life, and many mind mountains in business!

This is my journey...

My parents taught me from a young age, that you can achieve anything you want, with hard work and dedication. Coming from a very spiritual mother, it was no surprise to find myself working towards a career of holistic well-being. Be kind, always and treat everyone as you'd like to be treated. Great advice from my parents, as I started my journey on the road to becoming a therapist.

My mother loaned me £2,000 to buy my first piece of equipment. I was working part time in a beautiful old hunting lodge, that had been converted into a health and fitness club and running beauty salon events in people's homes, to earn enough money to open up this one room at Ambassadors.

And finally, the day came, 17th July 1993, after completing my three year qualification. I worked for two years on my own and then employed my first therapist, Georgina, who went on to work with me for 14 years. I've always been someone with a plan and set my business and personal intentions every year. I went on to employ another two therapists.

We went on to expand the salon and take on another two treatment rooms, with four in total. 15 years ago, we bought our own property, Apple Orchard Cottage and Village Post Office.

We really started to put our salon on the map and locally became known for our professionalism and outstanding customer care. The next five years involved taking on more therapists a reception team and marketing, plus the beginning of our entries into national and local awards .

We won our first award in 1999, which put us on the road to maintaining and setting very high standards. We maintained a level headed approach and realised that winning awards, brings attention on your business but it is only a moment in time and you can't sit back on your laurels, as you are as only as good as your last treatment. We have won 48 awards to date.

Being a therapist, has never been a job, it's definitely a passion and I have always felt honoured that people trust you with so much information about themselves. One of the early rules I made at Beauty Time and taught my team, was that at all times you must follow the professional code of conduct, if you want to be taken seriously.

Clients relationships that have been founded through Beauty Time, must always be treated with the utmost respect. Although clients will appear to be friends, due to the nature of the one-to-one relationship, the privacy of both client and therapist must be maintained at all times.

As social media has grown and it's easy to be a fly on the wall of people's lives, it's more important than ever to protect and respect the Client/Therapist relationship.

Giving back to others, brings a sense of grounding when you work in a luxury industry. I decided to work with charities close to the hearts of my clients and as the reputation of the salon grew and our working relationship with companies and product houses flourished, this enabled us to offer raffle prizes as incentives. I took on my first challenge and walked on the Great Wall of China and raised thousands for the NSPCC. As the years went on, I jumped out of planes, wing walked, did a double marathon, trained with the SAS, climbed Machu Picchu and recently climbed Base Camp Everest to name but a few challenges.

I was invited to the Queen's Garden Party in June 2019, to celebrate the money I had raised, which was a huge surprise and honour.

Blessed with not being overly nervous in front the camera, or a microphone, I have often been asked to present on both television and radio. I think when you are passionate, it's just a case of sharing that love and enthusiasm for what you do.

Many people know that I am a Buddhist by faith and have lived in many monasteries throughout the world, and this has given me an insight into compassion and kindness. I took my own Buddhist vows in 2016, with Lama Yeshe, at Samye Ling Tibetan Monastery and then went on to study and become, a meditation teacher with the British School of Meditation. I now offer my own meditation classes, online classes, forums and four-day retreats.

This insight into the mind, has made me understand that

mind fitness, is the key to understanding yourself and what limits you, or inspires you, to push on, even when things are tough. As therapists, we are often listening to stories of client's lives. I could see that teaching meditation through my business, would not only help clients feel more relaxed, it could also help to keep them mentally stronger and younger.

Always aim to be someone your team can look up to, never ask anything of them that you are not willing to do yourself, invest in them, show them their worth. It goes without saying that sometimes you will employ people that are not a natural fit in your team and business, these are the difficult times, when you have to be brave. Respect that the team members who give all to you, deserve to work in a healthy and productive environment. I've been fortunate to have had longevity with many of my team, on average many have worked for me over 15 years. I have always supported and encouraged my therapist to enter awards and many have gone on to win national awards themselves. Entering awards as an individual, isn't for everyone but the girls who stand centre stage in your business, understand that without the support of the team and reputation of the salon, winning is not possible, as each supports the other.

You invest a lot of time, love and energy into your teams and you will be there with them on some of the most precious days of their lives. Wedding days, baby days and sometimes sad days...

They become like family to you and often, just as important as your own close family. One of the hardest lessons by far, is learning to let go, when the time comes for them to move on and to wish them luck, as they begin the next chapter in their own life. Then look back and be thankful for the days, years and times, they gave to you and your business.

Finding the right people for the right job is key. The customer journey, expectation and excitement, comes from the first mention of your business, whether it is by word of mouth, recommendation, search engines or social media. That first phone call, that first opening of the door to your salon, is vital to the lasting impression you leave in the mind and experience of the clients. Our reception team have always been outstanding.

You learn a lot about yourself managing a team and when we have had girls in the team that haven't been suitable, or we have had to let go, due to salon standards not being met, you realise more than ever that your own mental health is important. Trying to be kind, with dignity and not becoming tangled up in becoming defensive, are hard lessons to learn at first but you begin to realise, that some will treat their role in your business as just a job, whilst others will match your own passion and it will definitely be a career.

You have to stay focused and see what is right for your business. If your clients have been visiting your salon for many years, it is the standards and professionalism that will keep them coming back, year after year. You must always seek to find and invest in people with your own visions. For the right people, the rewards and job satisfaction are clear to see and this is where the synergy of the right therapists in the right role and great business, is the perfect match and will result in years of wonderful employment and personal growth for both.

Thank you to team members and clients who have been on this journey and continue to still believe in the magic of Beauty Time.

I started my journey as a Beauty Therapist, then became an Holistic Practitioner, National Judge, Industry Advisor, Government Trailblazer and Vice President to the FHT. Meditation Teacher and I am now, a Wellbeing Retreat Master. Understanding where to diversify and when you need to grow personally, is like climbing a mind mountain, but when you reach the top and can see it all so much clearer, you know that every step was worth taking, even if you had to rest for a while and catch your breath.

If you are looking ahead to your own next mind mountain, or challenge, may you be better equipped and mentally prepared for that journey, having read in this book, the accounts of some of the most amazing women in our industry.

Always remain focused and brave ....

Millie xx

PS. Don't forget to be kind to yourself I have taught many the power of buying yourself The Goddess Gift anything to just say well done a bunch of flowers, bar of chocolate or even a Hermes scarf (a little extreme, lol), but we had just won Professional Beauty Salon of the Year, for the third consecutive year!

About Maria Mason

Maria Mason is recognised as one of the UK's top Professional wellness industry influencers with awards for business and leadership. With expertise that spans no less than 30 year, she is the owner of Salon of Excellence Beauty Time Bristol, the first salon to win the  coveted title Professional Beauty UK Salon of the Year for three consecutive years. The team has won more than 48 awards to date.

Maria is Vice President to the Federation of Holistic therapists, a National Judge of ten years to the professional beauty industry, presenter on TV and radio, writer for tabloid and trade publications, speaker and mentor. She has an unwavering passion, enthusiasm and dedication to the holistic beauty industry.

She is holistic practitioner qualified in over 15 therapies, mind fitness meditation teacher, retreat master - the complete Mind Body Practitioner.

She has a personal passion for mountain climbing and a deep faith in Buddhism, having combined the two recently trekking in the Himalayas to base camp Everest.

Her vision is to inspire others on their own personal journey to inner health and strength through meditation. She offers personalised meditation programs, to the corporate world and one to one personal development all available through her online platforms, retreats, workshops and classes.

Contact Maria

beautytime@btconnect.com

www.beautytimemariamason.co.uk

Facebook Beautytimebristol

Instagram BeautytimeBristol

I Had A Dream

Brenda Kingswood

I loved going for beauty treatments and dreamt one day I would love to have my own Beauty Salon or Spa. I loved the way having a treatment was such a positive experience and made me feel so good I wanted to share this experience with others.

Driving home from work one day in the summer of 2000, I saw a To Let sign appear on a beauty salon in a desirable part of town and thought this could be it – I arranged a viewing – the salon was in a state of disrepair – no sinks in the rooms, stained carpet on the floor and so on but I thought *I can make a go of this,* so, I agreed to take on the lease and handed in my notice. This meant giving up a senior manager's position in a Training Company with a company car where I had worked for 11 years. I had created many opportunities for the company but also for myself and felt that I had come as far as I could and it was time for a change – yes a total career change or late life crisis at 52 years old call it what you like!

When people found out that I was going to open a beauty

salon they thought I had lost the plot and they were probably right! However, unbeknown to everyone I had actually been going to night classes to learn how to do treatments i.e. waxing, manicures, pedicures, nail extensions and massage and I had experienced enough facials in my time to know what was a good facial or not so if the opportunity to own my own salon or spa ever arose I would be in a better position when managing staff if I knew exactly what was expected of them and what standards I wanted them to deliver.

I arranged for a shop fit stripping the whole salon back to a shell as it was in such a terrible state. I recruited staff and took on Clarins, Environ, Aromatherapy Associates and CACI.

In September 2000, Savannah Beauty Centre was born — it was so so exciting.

One of the main aspects in my previous role was organising and delivering women's personal development training and customer care courses. Prior to my leaving, I had been in the process of organising a Women's Conference for approximately 150 women. I had managed to secure Heather Mills as the keynote speaker, which was a real coup because at that time she was married to Paul McCartney and very much in vogue. I had heard her speaking at a conference and was very impressed with her story - her amputation and how she had overcome this disability and her amazing charity work. Heather had received many accolades and awards including a nomination for The Nobel Prize. My employers asked if I would still continue to organise this — so as well as opening a new salon I agreed I would continue to finalise this conference which was due to take place in a couple of weeks!

Heather flew in from New York for the event and the company got lots of brilliant press coverage for this because of her high profile. The conference was a huge success ending on a high with everyone belting out, *Sisters Are Doing it For Themselves*. And I left the company on a high!

Back to building up a business. Two years after opening the salon I was invited to set up and operate a spa in a new four-star hotel in the city centre which had amazing pool and leisure facilities, but no treatment rooms.

I grabbed the opportunity; after all I had always wanted a spa. I converted three sunbed rooms into treatment rooms because they weren't purpose-built treatment rooms nor were they the luxurious spa rooms I had envisaged. I had converted them, as best I could, into lovely treatment rooms. Clients had the full use of the pool facilities, and we offered fantastic spa packages with amazing food. The combination just worked so well – this was another huge success. As an added bonus, within the hotel they had luxurious apartments which I was able to hire and recreate more treatments rooms, when needed.

At that time, the hotel was privately owned and the owners approached me about setting up and running a spa for them in their hotel in Fort William, Scotland. I considered the idea but the journey was about three hours drive and not on the best of roads. Winter time, logistically, would have proved a challenge, so I declined.

Over the years, quite a few people have approached me about running their salons or spas for them, since.

The industry has changed so much during the last 20 years and nothing more so than advertising e.g. Facebook and

Instagram didn't exist. Online advertising wasn't available. Advertising was off line and I did a lot of costly newspaper, magazine and radio advertising.

When I decided to have a taxi advert, with a full length graphic along the side of the taxi, I had to get permission from the Council! I had a picture taken of one of my therapists having a hot stone massage which showed her lying face down with her back exposed with hot stones placed on it. The Council rejected it saying it was *too sexy!* Well, in publicity terms that was the best free advertising that ever happened to me because Savannah made full front page news in the *Glasgow Evening Times* ... *with* a copy of the picture we had submitted and a headline that screamed BANISHED! I could not have paid for that advertising. We were in *every* national newspaper! It was unbelievable. And the positive publicity we got was absolutely fantastic. People couldn't believe the council's draconian decision.

Of course, I appealed their decision and was then granted permission, which was brilliant. Seeing that picture promoting my business on a taxi as well as on huge digital billboards was amazing and made me feel so proud.

I believe staff development and training is crucial in any industry but with hands-on, like ours, even more so. Within a short time of opening, we were awarded *Investors in People* and I believe we were the first salon in the UK to achieve this honour and award.

I remember one member of staff who joined me straight from college. I noticed her passion, enthusiasm and her knowledge of treatments. She really impressed me. I saw so much potential in her to create a role as a staff trainer as it didn't seem to matter what staff I employed I had to spend so much time training them to get them up to our salon standards. Numerous staff have said to me over the years they learned more working for me in three months than what they did at college in three years which is a lovely, compliment, but very concerning – but that's another story!

I decided to give this therapist the opportunity to become the staff trainer and enrolled her on various courses such as Training the Trainer, and it really paid off – she was with me for a long time. I am proud to say she now lectures in Beauty Therapy.

It was strange how my third salon came about 12 years ago. A member of staff travelled to work nearly an hour each way – a very loyal and a good, proficient therapist. She approached me and asked me if I would consider opening a salon in her area as there were no decent salons - mainly because she was finding the travelling a bit much. I thought, *Why not?* I am a great believer in *things happen for a reason* and the Law of Attraction.

There was a lovely town nearby called Bridge of Allan and I thought *wouldn't it be nice to have a salon there?* Very few shops come up for rent in this town, however, one did and I put an offer in for it, but wasn't successful. A couple of weeks later a new client came into the salon and she mentioned that she had come from Bridge of Allan, which surprised me as it is nearly an hour away from the salon.

I told her I had just submitted an offer for a shop in Bridge of Allan as I would like to open a salon there, but hadn't been successful. The next morning, I received a phone call from this client informing me that her friend had a salon in Bridge of Allan and she was interested in selling... and would I be interested. I contacted her friend, arranged to see the salon the next day, sealed the deal and became proud owner of salon no 3 all in a weekend!

The therapist worked there for a few years but her personal circumstances changed dramatically, so she had to give up her job and move away. I was disappointed as I had hoped she would build up the salon like her own and then we could come to some arrangement where she could eventually own it. I recently sold it after 12 years.

Probably, for me, the most interesting part of my story is when I was previously delivering a course on personal development two years before I opened my first salon. I asked the group to write down and draw a picture of their goals – I decided to do the same.

On that course, I drew a picture of myself and my family all looking very happy, standing in front of a salon. I kept that picture on my bedside table and a statement that read:

In two years, I will own my luxurious Beauty Salon
in the Milngavie/Bearsden area.

And guess what? That's exactly what happened! So, the moral of this story is:

Always follow and believe in your dreams – they do come true!

About Brenda Kingswood

Brenda is a successful entrepreneur and a fun loving person with a positive attitude and great sense of humour. Born and brought up in Edinburgh, she loves life. In her corporate role, Brenda completed a Diploma in Marketing, various management courses and Training the Trainer which helped enhance her career in customer care, administration and organisational skills but particularly in her specialist fields of women's personal development,.

Brenda's entrepreneurial spirit meant she always wanted to own her own business which she achieved later in life enjoying success with her own spas and salons.

Brenda is married with a hugely supportive husband. They have two sons. One lives in Barcelona with his partner and the other is married with three lovely children.

Contact Brenda

administrator@savannahbeautycentre.com

https://www.savannahbeautycentre.com

instagram – Savannah Beauty Centre

+44 0141 334 0077

Embracing Life's Challenges

Catherine Whelan

I was born in Cameroon, a country constantly in transition with a completely different social and cultural outlook. In the newly independent country things were continually changing. I can say with certainty, I belong to the generation of African women that witnessed one of the biggest feminist revolution of all time on a continent where women were longing to find their purpose.

My mum was a type of entrepreneur in her days. She started by building properties and selling them. She bought and sold merchandise. She was a real hustler. Sometimes, she would take me with her, and I would watch her cutting deals with all types of people. All that looked like hard work to me. I guess that is how I was unwillingly exposed to business, but I did not realise it for years.

You see, my mum did not get past primary school. In her days, after primary school, girls who were lucky enough went to a preparatory school ran by missionaries to learn how to cook, be a good wife and home maker. That is the only form of education she had.

My Dad considered himself lucky to get a scholarship to study dentistry in France, which was a rare opportunity in those days.

For my parents, education was everything. It was the key to freedom, success, and a privilege that many did not have. We were taught to take our education very seriously.

I had an amazing childhood doing many the things very few women generations before me could not do. I was captain the national basketball team and had the privilege of representing my country in various competitions.

After my studies, I received a foreign language degree in French and English, along with an MA in American literature and civilisation. Later, I was awarded a scholarship to study for another MA in translation and interpreting at a UK University where I met my husband and started a family. Nothing to do with beauty!

With four children, life became complicated. Juggling life and work was never easy and I worked freelance, in order to bring up a young family, make it to the school gate on time and cook family meals.

During those years, I just worked hard, with virtually no time for myself, but with a constant feeling that something was missing. In 2008, when the recession hit, there was less and less work. So, for a bit of extra money, I joined a company that was introducing women to skincare. I fell in love with the industry. I could see how women affected by stress enjoyed the sessions. I often felt drawn to go to beauty college for some formal training, but I could not find the time or the courage to make the change.

I would never have taken the dive without an unfortunate event that shook my family in the summer of 2008. Our 18 year old son passed away, very suddenly whilst on holiday in Spain with some friends. I felt numb with pain and totally broken but I could almost hear a voice from deep within nudging me to keep going.

At the same time the most surprising thing happened, I was not afraid anymore. I went to the local college that September, still grieving and enrolled on a Level 2 in beauty later specialising in Spa. People said I was crazy to leave a lucrative career behind, but nevertheless I carried on. Studying was very therapeutic for me and marked a great turning point in my life.

After graduation, I struggled to find job at my age in this industry. I needed experience so I was offered £3.50 per hour to work flexible hours in a beauty salon. I knew I was worth more, but I took it.

My career did not start out very well, just after a few months, I allowed too much wax to drip over a client's brow. It was a treatment I had done successfully numerous times but this one ended up in disaster, and needless to say, I was fired!

Lesson learnt, I was now beginning to understand the difficulties of working in the beauty and spa industry. Low salaries to start up with, not enough jobs for over 40s, so I asked myself: *Why don't you start your own business?*

So, I did! I rented a treatment room in the back of a chiropody practice and as I felt okay, I seized the opportunity to move to bigger premises just 18 months after. *How difficult could it be anyway?* I thought?

With one of my best friends on board sure we would hack it! Let me just say, it is never a good idea to do something like this, unless you are prepared to learn and learn fast! I have heard before that ignorance is bliss. Trust me ignorance is *not* bliss when the bills need to be paid.

I will always be thankful for the people God sent to help me set up the business. The people who gave us the money, the people who sold precious jewellery to see us start, the people who gave us the advice we needed and those who sacrificed their time to bring our ideas to life. That was only the start of journey of serious hard work.

I worked so hard in the treatment room for little to no salary, for many years. It was all about paying staff and paying the bills and there never seemed to be enough money to cover everything. Additionally, I had no time for admin or anything else.

One day my rent was late, and the landlord called me in and asked who was running the business while I was giving treatments. That made me seriously think...

I needed to find an answer to many questions, what was I doing wrong? A friend of mine recommended a book titled: *E Myth Revisited* by Michael E Gerber. It was an eye opener. I then realised I needed to take responsibility for this business and learn how to run it properly, and very quickly.

Here are the top five things that made the most impact on my business and that I can strongly recommend.

1. **Find a community of like-minded people who are facing the same problems as you.** I made sure I attended Professional Beauty (PB) regularly.

Attending PB was life changing for me, I met many other business owners and attended seminars where an invaluable amount of knowledge was shared. That has been my lifeline over the years and the place where I met most of my business mentors.

Get a mentor or as many mentors as you can.

Keep searching and you will find the right one for you.

2. **Find how to communicate with your staff and what motivates them.** Staff were the greatest challenge for me, but also my most important asset. It is essential that you invest in understanding and developing them. I learnt that lesson in my early days after losing virtually all the members of my original team in the space of three months, after they had been with me for just under two years. You want them to know what you need from them. By creating win/win situations all the time, you are sure to retain them for much longer. Regular team meetings and one-to0-ones can keep you close to your team.

3. **Define the values of your business clearly, to facilitate decision making and to staff alignment.** You want everyone to engage with your values and your beliefs, the guiding principles of your business.

4. **Develop systems and processes** so your business can run like a well-oiled machine without you. I had a mentor who encouraged me to list every job that needs doing regularly. You must write how to perform every process that your business requires with as much detail as possible. It is strange how even cleaning can be a challenge for some members of staff.

5. **Finally, commit to the process.** When we start a business, a lot of us think success will come overnight. It takes time! I allowed that reality to sink. That is when I started enjoying my journey the most. If you can commit to doing the right things one day at a time, you will build a strong foundation for your business.

Some days, I wanted to quit. When the bills were not paid, payments to suppliers were late or when I could hardly pay myself. Stay calm, and just make sure you talk to your suppliers. More often, than not they are quite understanding, everything always ends up working out for good.

Do not quit, just allow the process to equip you. There are no shortcuts.

Challenges are still present as we currently fight a pandemic. I am still moving forward, but with so much more confidence. I have learnt to embrace my challenges. Business is surely more like a marathon. Only those who show endurance will eventually find success.

About Catherine Whelan

Catherine Whelan is a co-founder of Spa Beautiful, a property of Wellness & Beauty for All C.I.C. created in 2012 and turned into a Community Interest Company in 2017.

Catherine Joined the spa Industry in 2004 after a 20-year career as a linguist. She has spent the last 4 years studying Spa Management at The University of Derby. Her research focuses on staff retention. She is passionate about creating a healthy work environment and building a company that helps to uplift people with excellence.

Catherine believes that beauty and spa treatments have a strong positive impact on our mental health. Her holistic approach includes life coaching and talking therapies to serve her community in a meaningful way, all while helping to connect them to true beauty within.

Born in Cameroon, West Africa she has lived in the UK for over 30 years. She lives with her family in Cheshire.

Contact Catherine

https://www.linkedin.com/in/catherine-whelan-35296631

Yes! This Is Working!

Sarah Atkinson

This is the story of my journey from therapist, to salon owner, to *The Post Lady*. And a few lessons I learned along the way.

Beauty therapy is something I fell into. I thought it would be fun and a quick ticket out of my small town – to adventure overseas!

After my initial training in New Zealand, I signed up to work on cruise ships. This would be my first time leaving my home country, and I was excited. I had no idea what to expect, or what I was getting myself into. But I was ready for new experiences.

My mum was very adventurous in her younger years. She had backpacked around the world and seen so many places. She would always share her inspiring adventures and stories with us growing up. So, from a young age I had a sense of adventure and interest in other cultures.

I didn't know what to expect – I'd never been on a cruise ship before.

It was a whole new world – many different people from all over the world. Working in the spa was an experience! I learned so much in a short period of time. It was very much – sink or swim, and I took on the challenge. Retailing was an important part of the job. I was the best retailer on all three of the ships I was on. It was great to be admired by my colleagues. Because of this I was part of a hand-picked team to travel to Italy to meet a brand-new ship, set up the spa, and sail across the Atlantic to America, passenger free. This was a treat and the spa itself was so beautiful and luxurious.

On the ships, I met an Irish friend – and this is how I ended up coming to Ireland. I came to Ireland with a one year working holiday visa, that turned into 15 years.

After six years of managing a great salon, I felt it was time to go out on my own. It was a little scary at first, but I had a feeling that it would work out. I wanted to be in control of my destiny.

At this point, myself and my partner decided to take a year off and go to Thailand to teach English. This was an amazing year, and the experience was invaluable. While I was in Thailand, I was excited to get back and start my business. Being in Thailand reinforced what I already believed – we have to take all the chances and opportunities we're given in life. In the western world we're given a lot. Make the most of what you've got – the possibilities are endless.

Back in Ireland myself and a friend started our salon.

I'll never forget the first phone call. The first lady wanted an eyebrow shape.

We were jumping up and down — so excited at our first client! I felt great. I felt like — *Yes! This is working!* Getting that first booking was a feeling I'll never forget. I felt unstoppable in that moment.

The first year or so, was tough and we got most of our clients through word-of-mouth and old-fashioned marketing.

I have learned some valuable business lessons.

Getting Clients Is The Hard Part,
And The Most Important Part

We needed to get fully booked. I worked with a couple of business coaches, but what I really needed was the bookings. I ended up doing some Facebook marketing training, and this is when my business took off.

Don't Forget Why You Started

I had opened a second location because I was in the *hustle hard* mindset. I had fed into the idea that you were either growing or dying. You always had to be expanding and getting bigger to be successful. At the time the popular opinion with business coaches and success gurus was — *hustle hard or go home.* I was working way too many hours, for honestly — little return. It did *look good* to have two locations, but I was wearing myself out trying to do everything.

One day I was thinking about how tired I was. *Was I even happy? Why wasn't I happy?*

I had become extremely busy... *being busy.*

It was because I had gotten so far off the path of what I

actually wanted out of the salon. I had originally wanted a money-making machine, that was easy to run and manage, so I could have lots of free time to do other things, outside of work. But I had gotten caught up in what I thought I *should be doing*. But they weren't my goals. I was choosing to work so much – *for someone else's dream and vision*.

So, I decided to get rid of the second location (it was a financial drain and didn't take off as I thought it would). I also decided to cut back down the menu and specialise. This would be easier to market, the salon would run very smoothly if only a few treatments were being done, and we would be known as the specialists in these three treatments, which would look better in the client's eyes. I decided on Lash Lifts, Hollywood waxes and Microdermabrasion facials. This took a weight off my shoulders and I felt happier and more focussed.

Be Different, Don't Try To Be Better

One of the first, and best bits of business advice I got was – *Be different, don't try to be better. Everyone says they're the best. You need to be different.*

We were very busy, and things were running smoothly, but I felt like I wanted us to be different from all the other salons. I didn't want to blend in or be *just another salon.*

I was wanting to make the business really stand out somehow and be different. I put it out there, I decided this is what I wanted. I knew an answer would come to me.

And one day, shortly after, I was walking down the street and the name hit me – *Late Night Beauty Salon.*

My eyes widened – *OMG yes!*

I ran back to the salon and bought the domain name. I quickly downloaded a business name change form and filled that out. Within 30 minutes of the name coming to me – we were on our new journey as *Late Night Beauty Salon*.

I was so excited. I could envision the logo, the colours, everything.

I knew that clients would say – *Oh wow – that's such a good idea. No one else is doing this.*

We were very successful with the new name and branding. It got us recognised by different online blogs and magazines.

No one else was doing late nights. We had been super busy and had recently started offering really late appointments – until 10pm, and our clients loved and appreciated this. I thought it was cool, very New York, busy city vibe.

So, I guess there's another lesson there – trust your gut and act fast.

For me, the most exciting part of the business was always, getting bookings. Getting fully booked and having a waiting list. This was when I felt secure in the business. I felt successful and proud of my business.

That feeling of excitement I got from our first ever booking, has never left me, and this is the inspiration for my marketing business. I want to give people the feeling that, *Yes, this is working!*

Now, I help salon owners with their social media – all of it's based on my own experience and what I did to build my salon via Facebook.

I had originally done a Facebook marketing course a few years previously and discovered that I had a skill for post writing. Other people on the course asked me to write posts for them, I did, and they got lots of bookings.

I never dreamed I could do it full time and help salon owners all over the world! And now I'm known as *The Post Lady!*

At the start I had a feeling that this would really help people, and there was no one else focusing solely on posts to get bookings. There were lots of business coaches – but I wanted to specialise.

It's always good to be different, right?

Plus, this was what I was best at. I started out by doing a few posts for people in a Facebook group, and a course, to test it out. I had hundreds of responses! I had amazing feedback from people who got lots of bookings from the posts I did. At this moment I felt again, *Yes! This is working!*

I feel that writing posts and seeing the results that my clients get, is my true passion. I can relate to them and it's very rewarding when you're helping someone to build their business, and their life. I know what it means.

It's that spark of creation, a spark of endless possibilities, success and fulfilled dreams!

This is why we start our businesses.

Over the years I have learned a lot. All the best things happened when I followed my gut and trusted myself. I believe that we are powerful creators and there are no limits. I say, if you have an idea, just go for it. Enjoy the journey and celebrate the *Yes! This is working!* moments.

About Sarah Atkinson

Sarah Atkinson has been in the beauty industry for 21 years. She started out as a therapist working on cruise ships, moving on to managing a busy salon, to owning her own salon, *Late Night Beauty Salon*. Sarah now helps fellow salon owners with their marketing needs and is known as *The Post Lady*.

Sarah originally trained in New Zealand where she gained CIBTEC, ITEC and CIDESCO qualifications. She also has an Honours Degree in Social Science.

Her salon *Late Night Beauty Salon* has gained recognition from popular national publications, blogs and influential websites.

Sarah has a passion for sharing her experience and knowledge with others.

She is currently based in Dublin, Ireland and is mum to Missy, a beautiful Whippet Cross.

Contact Sarah

info@doneforyousalonposts.com

www.doneforyousalonposts.com

https://www.facebook.com/groups/1639595936107020

https://www.instagram.com/done_for_you_salon_posts

Reach For The Moon
But Aim For The Stars

Susanne Webb

What an amazing world we live in. A world that, if we just stopped a while to look, is simply bursting with opportunities. Some we choose to reach out with both hands and grasp, whilst others we choose to let slip away to be lost forever or perhaps to be revisited when the time seems right. With affection, I like to imagine that life can be compared to a bowl of exotic fruit with its centre a punnet of delicate and super-sweet raspberries and its outer ring a circle of eye-wateringly spiky prickly pears.

My story begins in West Africa where I was born and raised along with my two sisters and brother. As with most expat families, boarding school was a necessity. So, at the tender age of eight and a half, I joined my siblings in Scotland, returning to Nigeria for our wonderful school holidays.

I believe it was through the incredible experiences whilst living in that far-flung land that I found my love of fascinating faces, striking colours, flamboyant people, and the exhilarating rhythm of Afrobeat music.

Choices, Choices?

How do you even begin to decide on your future career path when there are so many to choose from?

When I was young and there were career choices to be made, I had on my list: Art College, Interior Design College, and Beauty College - all of which I was accepted for but with the advice and support of my parents, I chose Beauty Therapy as my future career. And to this day I am so thrilled that I did. I came to this surprisingly mature and sensible decision because not only did Beauty embrace my young emerging skill set but – even at the tender age of 17 – I understood that this growing industry was beginning to gather pace and momentum. And that, most importantly within the title of Beauty Therapy, there were many offshoots that potentially could continue to satisfy my passions, development and independence for the foreseeable future.

So, what makes us choose the direction we eventually decide to follow?

I believe it's a combination of many situations and events. Most often we make our choices due to family influences and pressures, our own personal experiences, and our inherited gifts. Above all, I believe we are driven to choose our individual paths by our natural instinct, desires, and passions.

If you were to ask me for one word of advice, without a moment of hesitation I would say *Qualifications!* Choose your

College with the utmost of care but above all choose your level of qualification wisely. For without the highest level of qualification to suit your abilities and aspirations, your career could quite possibly have disappointing limitations. I achieved CIBTAC and CIDESCO levels of training, and in doing so have had the opportunity to specialise in Medical Aesthetic Treatments. If I had so desired, these qualifications would have enabled me to work whilst travelling the world.

Thirty-five years ago, when I first began my journey into the world of Beauty, there were very few salons and even fewer Beauty Colleges. So, from Scotland I headed to Bretlands Beauty College in Kent, England, under the watchful eye of the formidable yet inspiring Joan Thornycroft. Mrs Thornycroft ruled her kingdom with a rod of iron and skilfully educated her pupils that standards matter, that efficiency matters, and that meticulous hygiene matters.

To this day, each and every lesson I learned from her I still hold high as an ever-present badge of honour and gratitude.

So Let's Fast-Forward

You are now a fully qualified Beauty Therapist, and eager to introduce yourself to your universe of clients.

As your literary mentor, I invite you to grab a chair and come sit with me and I will share with you some of the best kept secrets of not only how to be a *Beauty* but also how to be the very *Best of Beauties!*

The connection with your client should begin the instant they pass the threshold of your salon, and only end when they leave floating on air feeling as though for those few precious hours, they are the only person in the whole universe that really matter.

As the owner of a boutique-style salon, my greatest joy is to see those contented clients laden with homecare products, their future six-month appointments well and truly booked, and the widest and most infectious smile radiating for all to see.

Some clients love to chat but others come to you when seeking sanctuary from life's everyday stresses and strains.

In truth... you have to be that confidential listening ear, that soother of worries, and when required that exuberant entertainer... but never that advisor, as advisors we most certainly are not!

Treatment Hints

Let's talk about facial treatments...

It may sound over-dramatic but you instinctively know when you have given the very best treatment possible because, to me, it feels like giving away a tiny bit of your very soul!

With skill, rhythm, and the ebb and flow of pressure, your hands glide with knowledge and understanding over the planes if your precious client's face.

To recognise and to have the ability to convey calm and well-being through your hands is a gift that I believe surpasses all others.

Let's talk about Medical Aesthetic Treatments...

For 27 years, I practiced Sclerotherapy in my salon – the truly remarkable treatment that removes veins and thread veins on legs by means of injections.

For the past 30 years I have dedicated most of my working week to Advanced Cosmetic Procedures – the removal of unwanted skin blemishes such as skin tags, warts, cysts, milia and much more.

For the past 35 years I have helped many clients with unwanted hair growth by offering Electrolysis, the only permanent method of hair removal.

Throughout those years I have always held the following two principles dear to my heart, and have often called upon them at times of client pressure.

- **Precision:** This is the high level of refinement with which a procedure is performed so that we always follow strict guidelines on technique and protocol.

- **Meticulous Hygiene:** As with all salon equipment and tools of your trade, pay the utmost attention to every detail of cleanliness. In doing so you protect both yourself and your client.

We strive for perfection in all we do!

If, at the end of your longest, most tiring and arduous of days, having attended to your most challenging of clients, you can truly say to yourself, *I have given 100% of my expertise, knowledge, and dedication,* you are with absolute certainty well on your way to a successful and fulfilling career.

Always Remember

And so, I move onto your Gold Star of self-training relayed in three easy steps:

- **Your smile** – your greatest asset or conversely your greatest downfall! Your smile should be completely genuine and its warm welcome should shine directly through to your eyes - they are after all *the windows to your soul*

- **Your eyes** – the correct level of eye contact conveys interest at what's being said, shows respect, and is an essential tool for delivering positive messages of confidence particularly during your client's first visit and consultation

- **Your posture** – without you realising, your body's posture is like a loudspeaker, signalling to all how you are really feeling, be it intimidated, anxious or unconfident...a certain recipe for disaster if you don't get it right!

So... relax those shoulders, lift up your chin, stop fiddling and stand up straight. Be proud of who you are and what you know.

My Wish And My Thanks

I was truly delighted to be chosen alongside 21 other leading salon owners to contribute to this wonderful *Beauty and the Best* book. The Beauty industry is most certainly here to stay and is growing by the day in both direction and strength.

My greatest wish is that I may have motivated and encouraged at least one reader to step forwards into the exciting world of Beauty.

I wish you all the very best of luck, and I look forward to reading about you in the Who's Who of Beauty.

Thank you. Xx

About Susanne Webb

Susanne is an Advanced Aesthetic Beauty Therapist with 35 years' experience. For the last 30 years she has been the proud owner of a fabulous boutique-style salon in Kent, England.

For 27 years Susanne specialised in Sclerotherapy. She also specialises in Advanced Cosmetic Procedures (ACP), Electrolysis, and Guinot skincare treatments. She is CIDESCO and CIBTAC trained.

In addition to her working week, Susanne is keen to spread the message of Beauty by giving inspiring and educational talks to both children in schools and ladies in community groups.

Susanne is happily married with a grown-up son, and a boisterous labradoodle puppy called Ricco.

Contact Susanne

susanne.webb24@gmail.com

https://www.pinebrae.com

https://www.facebook.com/pinebraebeautysalon

Dare To Dream

Stefania Rossi

My background is not in the beauty industry.

Owning a beauty clinic was a dream that I secretly cultivated for many years. I was attracted to the beauty industry from a young age and took a massive interest in it, without even considering that my passion could become a career and a new way of life for me.

And why not? Because all my background and qualifications were in restaurant management and contract funding management... I was forty years old... what sort of nonsense I was thinking!

My working career started in the hospitality industry in Sardinia (Italy) at the age of 16 years old. I relocated to London when I was 19 years old when I completed my Diploma in Foreign Languages and progressed with both my studies and my career into restaurant management and hospitality recruitment, recruiting for five-star hotels and restaurants in London for ten years.

I then joined what I call the *corporate world* and spent over ten years within the Learning and Skills sector, working in senior business management roles and particularly specialising in managing teams, contract performance, and business development and transformation. One job led to the other and I was beginning to feel like I was just going through the motions, and although I was driven by the profiles and responsibilities of the roles, I was not listening to my own interests and true passions.

I got to a point in my life when I tragically lost my sister, that made me re-evaluate my life, and gave me the determination to follow my heart and passion for the amazing beauty industry.

My sister, Lisa, was a very spontaneous person and the life and soul of everyone. She lived her life fully, like it was her last day and I can still hear her voice repeating these words to me, We *have one life, and it is short...choose how to live it.*

In the many years that I was cultivating my passion for the beauty industry, I loved everything about beauty, wellness, wellbeing, the feeling of being in a beauty salon and the happiness of being in this environment. So, for many years, I researched it by reading and studying it, visiting my friends that worked in salons, attending beauty and trade shows, signing myself up to all seminars I could and listening and learning from the *experts*.

I felt that I had transferrable skills, I loved managing teams, transforming, and developing businesses for other companies.

But this was the biggest decision of my life, the fear of walking away from job security, a good career and wanting to invest all my savings into my dream.

Eventually I felt ready to take on a new venture, owning my beauty clinic.

One morning, back in early 2013, I remember clearly walking into my CEO's office to resign as National Operational Director. I also walked away from a career of many years. The fear was becoming a roaring fire inside me and this transformed itself into a magical excitement... to follow my dream and an exciting new life.

It was a very scary thought, as there was no going back, but something that was beating inside my heart was stronger than I can explain. Something strong and magical was attracting me to the beauty industry. I needed to do it. I had to make it work, all my life savings were going into this.

I always wanted a business where I could make a difference as an employer and where I could also utilise my background in building and developing teams, where I could help others.

My desire was to be able to offer an environment of wellbeing and calmness for our clients making a difference in their lives, to make them look and feel their best.

So, after spending many months looking at salons, I bought Utopia in late 2013. I took on a massive challenge, as Utopia was a failing business and literally on its knees. However, I can proudly say that it has been the best choice I have ever made!

I fell in love with Utopia as soon as I walked in. Located in a fantastic High Street setting, the salon was based over three floors with nine treatment rooms. I saw it with the eyes of a mother, a baby that needed to take care of, and I saw a lovely team who needed nurturing and they were eager to nurture this baby with me but did not have the right tools and needed the guidance so that could succeed themselves.

It wasn't plain sailing and there were a few challenges along the way, many lessons learnt, but I had the fortune to have met the best experts that taught me so much.

My vision for the salon was to transform it into a highly reputable, successful salon in the area expanding to advanced skincare treatments, to develop the team to a highly trained and confident team and to provide them with progression routes and win the trust and loyalty of our clients as well as my own team.

I remember sharing my vision with the team that I wanted us to be an award-winning salon, too! They looked at me as if I was a crazy woman but could also see an exciting spark in their eyes.

I retained the whole team and within less than two years, Utopia has transformed from a failing salon into an award-winning salon. My first award was the very prestigious national award *Professional Beauty Employer of the Year, 2016.*

I remember walking onto the stage of the Professional Beauty Awards to pick up my award and saying to myself, *I have done it Lisa! Are you watching me from up there?*

Would my Mum and Dad even believe it? They made financial sacrifices to fund my studies and I wanted to make them proud that I was finally that successful employer and not working for someone else.

I wrote to all my previous employers letting them know... I wanted them to know that I did it and that it was not just a midlife crisis that I was going through!

For the last eight years at Utopia, we have continued working hard as a team, serving our clients, building trust and our profile, and we have won another eight national awards.

I continued to listen to that *voice*... and crazily enough I wanted more.

I was getting involved in national and international beauty industry campaigns to promote the opportunities in the hair and beauty industry. I was asked to speak at colleges and trade shows and talk about my journey. I was honoured to be asked to be an international judge for the beauty industry and adviser, and the more I participated the more I wanted to help and inspire as many people as possible to join this amazing industry.

I was always thinking, *What's next? Do I want to expand and open another salon?* But I always believed that things happen for a reason and I eventually found what my *next* was.

It was becoming clear to me in a very natural way that I really enjoyed helping employers with advice in finding the right talent for their business and wanted to help individuals finding new career paths. So, my recruitment background kicked back into life, and my own hair and beauty recruitment company was born, *Stefania Rossi Recruitment.*

My vision there was to support other salon owners in developing and building their teams with my very own formula, a personalized and tailor-made recruitment support.

Once again, I was incredibly grateful for what this industry was giving me and the endless avenues it can offer.

One thing I must be grateful for, is that I have been truly fortunate to have met incredible and inspiring people in this fantastic journey, that supported my dreams and believed in me.

It is so true, that it is important to surround yourself with inspiring people and what a difference it makes!

So after looking at the beauty sector gaps, it was clear the industry was shouting out that there was a massive shortage of talent in our industry. I saw an opportunity to support young talent in finding resources to upskill, help them become more attractive to employers and explore the many great opportunities available to them in the industry.

For many months I worked purely on what was a labour of love, and I developed an online platform called *Hidden Talent*, a *free* online resource centre, where individuals can develop and improve their skills, expand their knowledge with inspirational resources, and become more employable.

Hidden Talent generated much interest in Colleges and across the industry and I soon found myself promoting it nationally.

One key thing that I always say when I talk about the opportunities in the hair and beauty industry is that *this is not just a career, it is a lifestyle.*

There is no magic winning formula that I can share; the key is that I have always loved developing and surrounding myself with good teams, and I have been fortunate in this.

My advice now to anyone is, anything you want to do, make it your passion; become an expert in your field.

You can have a true enjoyable and rewarding career. Give it your All. Really value yourself as no one will shout louder than you, about yourself, apart from you.

The beauty industry has certainly been the Best for me... and it has only been eight years so far!

Here's to you... your future, your success. Follow your heart, your dreams, and grasp the moment. Persevere. You can achieve anything you want.

Believe and focus on your dream and in what you want to achieve.

Dare to dream that the impossible... is possible.

About Stefania Rossi

Stefania Rossi is originally from Italy but has lived in the UK since she was 19. She is a multi-award winning salon owner who prides herself on her ability to motivate, retain and develop great teams. She has combined her extensive business management skills with specialist recruitment skills to create *Stefania Rossi Recruitment*, an international recruitment agency, for the hair and beauty industry. It solves a key challenge that most salon owners face: finding talented stylists and therapists. *Hidden Talent*, a unique free resource, takes support for salon owners to a whole new level. It helps to upskill new and existing employees, and combines recruitment and training services, offering a highly successful, value adding service that matches the perfect salon candidate to the right employer.

Through her passion for the industry Stefania has become a sought-after international speaker and awards judge, industry advisor, mentor, and regular expert contributor to articles on recruitment, training and careers in health and beauty.

Contact Stefania

stefania@stefaniarossi.co.uk

www.stefaniarossi.co.uk

www.wearehiddentalent.com

www.utopiabeautyandspa.co.uk

This Is Me

Jane Barker

I would like to share my journey with you. I have been a beauty therapist for 43 years. I am 61 and fortunately, have never been out of work. There have been some rocky times, always having something to do with a lack of self-confidence in reading, writing and maths. Later in life, it was recognized as dyslexia.

Not A Good Starting Point

I left school, not really knowing what I wanted to do. My parents were concerned for my future. I was not an academic. My youngest sister was more academic. I was sent to boarding school as they thought it would be better for me. My sister to a day school.

From that day on we lead separate lives.

I hated being away from home and my sister, Sue, wanted what I had; to be in boarding school. Eventually, I left school in 1977, aged 16, with no exams taken. I had left early. I was encouraged to enrol at a beauty school.

Fortunately, I had a friend who had an interview to attend a training school in South Shields, so I went along with Hillary and with our moms in tow! We went to the Continental School of Beauty Therapy and Cosmetology in Stanhope Road.

This was where it began.

There was a school with three rooms, a kitchen, a practical room, and a theory room in one part of the building, the beauty salon was next door. I used to travel there every day, taking three buses, occasionally being picked up by one of my parents to bring me home.

I loved my training. There were only nine students; the maximum would have been 12. Our teacher for everything was Pamela Riddle. She was amazing and knew that I had difficulties, especially with writing.

I worried about this a lot. *Would I be good enough? Would I pass my exams? Would I remember everything? Would I get a job? Would I earn enough? Would I have enough confidence? Would I fit in? What would I do if I didn't pass?*

The list was endless. Worry and anxiety are still part of my life today, but you learn to overcome and deal with them.

I have been employed in six salons but would like to pick out two that changed my life and filled me with determination and excitement for the future.

It was in 1979. I was 20. I went to work in *Clinic 54* in Grey Street, Newcastle upon Tyne. It was run by Frieda Bridgewood. She had a great happy business in my opinion, someone ahead of her time in the industry. She was a great networker and communicator. This was the first time

I had worked with more than two people. *Clinic 54* was in a fabulous old building over five floors. The first floor had the reception, hairdressing, beauty, showers, a sauna, waxing room and fast track treatment beauty chair and an enormous hydrotherapy bath. On the second floor was artificial nails, electrolysis, Guinot room body area, ultraviolet and sun beds. They had just come onto the market. The third floor was a model agency. The top floor had the staff room.

I always remember we were the first salon in Newcastle to offer fresh coffee, or at least that was what we were told. It was the first salon I worked at that had a receptionist. You have to remember there were no computers.

We had a till and a very large appointment book. I was always worried about taking money using the card machine and making appointments. Had I known, that I would have had to do this from time to time, I may never have accepted the job. It forced me to admit to them, that I could make dreadful mistakes. I could be brilliant one day and dreadful the next. Only with money and writing, I might add, but with their help, patience and understanding everything worked out well.

There were nine beauty therapists, about five hairdressers, I chiropodist and I receptionist.

Looking back on my time there, I suppose it was like a spa. Definitely the first of its kind. This salon was very busy and beauty was just becoming popular. I worked here for six years, so while it was sad to leave, I felt it was time to try and work on my own. Unfortunately, this did not work out.

My father died and this changed how I felt about life, my job, the future and everything.

What Happened Next?

Pamela Riddle rang me and asked could I help her out. She needed someone to teach electrolysis, part-time at Kirby College in Middlesborough. This was a great shock. I was terrified but said *Yes!* It was something different.

I cannot spell, I don't know the first thing about teaching, particularly a subject I had not practiced since I left training school.

Don't worry, she said, *we will sort all that out.*

After that, I did part time teaching for several years. During that time I went on to do a teacher training course 730 City and Guilds. Nothing about it was easy, but I passed. I went on to do more teaching at Peterlee College and at Hartlepool teaching nursery nurses Health and Hygiene.

While all this was going on, I also took a job in retail, selling a bronzing powder. I had never worked on the shop floor. It is amazing where life takes you.

I had wanted full time teaching but that never happened.

I was then asked if I would go back into beauty. After five years teaching, I had nothing to lose. This lead me back to the centre of Newcastle, with a company called Regis, inside a department store called Fenwicks. I was 32 years old and stayed for just under 21 years.

This was a totally different experience.

It was my first time working with a very large team. There were 18 beauty therapists and 22 hairdressers, not to mention receptionists and management. It was a very fast-moving salon, lots to do even more to learn, plenty of opportunities for training also you were responsible for understanding your weekly and monthly figures and had to hit your targets. Checking stock and lots of things I had never done before. Just the very size of it was frightening.

At one time I was doing three jobs: beauty therapist; beauty supervisor; and trainer. Beauty supervisor meant I had more responsibility, assisting the manager with stock control, ordering and lots more, training took me out of the salon. I met therapists that were new to the company and them to advance their skills and knowledge of how procedures in Regis were performed. All of these positions pushed me out of my comfort zone. You could say it gave me confidence and made me look for new challenges.

Time For Change

In 2014, I left Regis having enjoyed working with all the people, the experiences and the good times we had shared together. In hindsight, I should have left earlier.

Now I am self-employed and I work on the outskirts of Newcastle-Upon-Tyne. I have been there for nine years, alongside two friends, Julie, and her sister Debbie. They have worked together for 23 years in their own business. They have a warm, caring, team of experienced hairdressers and it's a salon filled with laughter and happiness. It always has a constant flow of tea or coffee, sometimes even wine and the occasional party.

I am fortunate to be a part of this. I have a quiet, peaceful space upstairs where clients have followed me from previous jobs. Working for myself has enriched my life and relaxed me. I find I now pass this new calm on to my clients through my treatments which are mainly facials, back massages, electrolysis, non-surgical facelifts and smaller treatments. It is wonderful to help improve people's confidence and well-being through a hands-on approach.

I believe in loving yourself first, giving the best of what you have to others and remembering to love and preserve everything that surrounds us to ensure a safer healthier future for the next generation. And the beauty industry is encouraging us to become greener, as well.

I have enjoyed my journey so far and wonder where it will take me next.

Thank you for taking the time to read this. I wish you well with your journey.

About Jane Barker

Jane Barker lives in Seaham on the North East coast of England where she has lived all her life. She has been a beauty therapist for 42 years, and has extensive experience. She has a Certificate for Teaching and has trained with over 13 different skincare companies. She has talked to many groups about beauty and at one time had a regular slot on a local radio station.

She is very interested in the youth of today and has ran youth groups for over 12 years.

Contact Jane

https://www.facebook.com/CACI-at-The-Beauty-Room-Newcastle-1617180425004373

Thirty Years And Counting

Dawn Stanley

I thought beauty was the path to perfection. My fantastic journey shows you my struggles and successes behind everything I have achieved and the sacrifices to get there.

I come from a small town called Accrington in North West England. Born to a hardworking Dad who had his own business, a snooker table fitter, making snooker tables for the rich and famous. Mum had obsessive compulsive disorder or Aspergers, so Dad took care of me.

My interest in beauty started age nine, attempting to make homemade perfumes. Then admiring fancy Nancy's nails up the street! She was the envy of every girl with her different coloured nails. I'd pester her for old makeup and excited when she gave me my first baby blue nail varnish.

My passion for beauty had begun! 'I always wanted to be a make up artist, but so did my friend, so I gave up on the idea. Always follow your dream and stick to it or have plan B and C like me.

Being a teenager, I wanted to go visit a sunbed shop. On entering, I felt a sense of calm, a place I belonged.

I was intrigued seeing beauticians tinting eyelashes. This could be the job for me! I applied for college but was heartbroken when I was turned down. They wouldn't take on 16 year olds.

I applied for the Government's Youth Training Scheme (YTS) and was so excited to be accepted into a beauty salon. It was a great experience working under an electrolysis expert. 12 months on I still wanted to go to College to get a full qualification. I asked my boss if she could keep me on as a Saturday girl and she agreed. I stayed with her whilst at college. We still keep in touch 30 years on and I always remember her - Andrea Catton Laser Clinic.

College was an exciting whole new level!

We went to beauty exhibitions in London and saw new treatments and machines about to hit the nation. I organised work experience and travelled all over the UK. I went to The Sanctuary Spa London, Piccadilly Hotel, Glemby Manchester, Barton Grange Health Spa, Brookland's Health Spa, Debenhams and a Yorkshire salon.

I dreamed of working on a cruise ship but deferred when my last placement Britannia Hotel Manchester offered me a job. Sadly, I had to leave Andrea and owe her so much. She gave me the knowledge and the confidence to take on the world!

Working in a hotel salon with a gym was an amazing feeling, especially meeting famous celebrities.

The work experience and college studies gave me the confidence and the determination, and I landed a job working for a chain of salons. Sadly, it didn't work out. What had I done wrong? I wasn't sure. My confidence was shaken. I felt so miserable! I felt like giving beauty up forever! But I slowly brushed myself off and asked my ex boss for my old job back. She was looking into renting a beauty room in a toning bed shop. Incredibly, she took me back on!

I introduced myself to clients, and started delivering treatments. When doing facials I'd close my eyes and think, *I wish this treatment room was mine!* Three months later, my boss asked if I would like to take it over. So my wish - and I had wished hard enough - came true!

I was one of the first to open in Darwen and this is where *Dawning Beauty* was born. I was 21 but felt ready!

Having started at 16, I had the passion to create the dream and I wanted this dream to work!

I would work all hours still making time to see my grandparents, who lived an hour away. At that time I split up with my partner and moved in with Mum as her carer.

I was asked to go on a cable TV interview about women in business, plus BBC Radio Lancashire. It was a fantastic feeling networking and speaking at women's events.

I met my new partner and he helped me greatly with the business ideas. Later we had two wonderful children. Three years on, we all had to move premises to the town centre. The business was growing so I decided to employ my first staff member. We instantly clicked and created a great client following. She stayed with me for 16 years. I was learning about payroll and accounts at night and carried out beauty treatments by day.

Two years later, my partner thought it was a good idea to

search for premises of my own. After three months of hard work my Greek themed salon was built. When we opened, it was a joyous event. We had a harpist playing in the day and a guitarist at night. I had the overwhelming support of my partner, family, friends and clients. Clients offered help with the buffet and my ex-boss turned up!

New clients soon came from far and wide. They liked our relaxed, unpretentious style that made them feel at ease. The first 30 seconds is key! My policy is: *Smile in a welcoming manner, like we've known them forever.*

Our second employee was 14, who started as a Saturday girl. When she turned 17, she studied beauty at college and now has her own salon and is enters Business Awards. I am so proud of her achievements.

The business had grown to a team of four when I fell pregnant. Sadly, a year later my partner and I split because he was fed up with my obsession to make my business thrive. I lived and breathed my business but hadn't realised.

Five years on we were a team of six.

In addition to the normal day-to-day business we also did (and still do) many special events like wedding fayres, business events and day trips out. As a team we've had many laughs and so much fun. It's the best journey ever!

I bought the shop next door to expand but then life events started to happen. Me and my partner got back together.

In 2005, I lost my Granddad and my Dad got cancer. The stress of running three properties proved too much when I fell pregnant again. I started working part time, juggling the family home, the business and managing staff.

I had far too much going on. Then my manageress fell pregnant, at the same time meaning both of us were off. There was no one steering the ship. I had put systems and processes in place and thought the business would run itself. How wrong I was!

The recession of 2008 was slowly making an impact without me realising! Client numbers started to dwindle and while I tried to boost client bookings, things overwhelmed me. I was, exhausted and sadly things broke down! I'd run out of ideas and motivation.

Three of my staff left. Two went to another salon. I replaced two staff but then had no clients. I was paying staffs wages but accruing huge debts. Things had spiralled out of control. It still makes me cry to think about it. It's hard to swallow even now. What a failure I'd become! I wish I had taken a step further back to see the bigger picture!

I regret taking on too many things at once, and not taking time to reflect. And for not asking for help. Thankfully, I had one member stay by me, becoming mangeress.

A few years on, things became more difficult as my partner had a heart attack then decided to leave. I went for counselling. My Mum died of cancer, and I was burgled six weeks later. My personal life was crashing down around me. I tried to rebuild the business but it was an uphill struggle. My existing manageress then left, after 14 years. I was devastated! I had no choice but to keep the business going for my family.

Going to the Professional Beauty exhibition I saw an article about Susan Routledge, a salon-owner mentor. I introduced myself and she has been a wealth of guidance and support ever since.

Right now I'm taking time to breathe, and to reflect on my journey. I'm slowly rebuilding my business with new staff and new treatments.

It feels like a new beginning, a new day. A new Dawn.

I am most grateful that I have loyal clients who have been with me, supporting me from the first day I opened almost 30 years ago! And I am grateful for the support of my family - my father and mother, stepmother, my dearest friends and even my ex. I'm grateful for all their support when I've needed it, at the times when it mattered the most.

But mostly, my children who have been through the ups and downs. I'm indebted and feel privileged to be surrounded by such caring patient and understanding people.

30 years on, the same clients come today. I must be doing something right.

I've always had a desire to teach, and then, who knows, go work on that cruise ship!

Anyone want to run the salon?

About Dawn Stanley

Dawn Stanley is a qualified salon owner of 30 years. The proud owner of *Dawning Beauty*, since 1991, she has employed and trained many staff who have gained qualifications, skills and experience enabling them to eventually teach or set up on their own.

Having qualified at Accrington and Rossendale College in Hair and Beauty, City & Guilds Level 3, and IHBC, Dawn prides herself on training staff to a high standard, and believing the highest accredited qualifications, apprenticeships and salon experiences are key to a long term professional success.

With extensive experience in salons and spas, she now enjoys electrolysis, red vein treatment, waxing, podiatry and pedicures. Her future plan is to gain a teaching qualification and implement better salon standards industry-wide.

Contact Dawn

dawn.stanley@hotmail.co.uk

https://www.dawningbeauty.co.uk

https://www.facebook.com/dawningbeautydarwen

https://instagram.com/dawningbeauty_darwen

Always Believe In Yourself

Anita Stubbings

I was 18 years old, and had just finished a two-year BTEC Diploma in Business and Finance. Having completed a three-week work placement in an office, I knew working at a desk 9-5 every day for the rest of my life was NOT for me and so, my journey into the beauty industry began!

In 1988, I enrolled at my local college for a one-year ITEC qualification in Beauty Therapy. This truly changed my life!

I loved every minute of it, and found something I truly excelled in. After qualifying, and working part time for a salon I decided to go it alone and set myself up as a mobile therapist. This is not for the faint-hearted. Back in the day you drove around from house to house: clients were not in; dogs, children (or both) were sniffing around your wax pot; or better still, Mrs X asking you to drink tea/wine and spend hours with her - all for the price of a lip wax!

I wanted more...

After a year or so of mobile, I was offered the opportunity to rent a room within a hairdressing salon. This was the first time I could really utilise my business qualification; setting up this small, but perfectly formed, room and to be able to offer all my beauty treatments under one roof. This was the start of the BodyMatters Empire!

I still wanted more...

In the mid 1990s, with an appetite for learning and discovery, I travelled to Texas (USA) on a vocational exchange programme to see how they operate across the pond by watching and working in salons and spas. This was truly an eye opener! Their beauty industry (back then) was poles apart from the industry in the UK. Many of their treatments were way behind ours. Although, I did bring a couple of ideas back home with me - just ask me about sugar and oil!

In 1999, I had my BIG break.

I was head hunted to take on the entire first floor of a manor house in a town centre location with space for four treatment rooms, above an established and ever growing hairdressing company. I jumped at this opportunity and became an employer. By the time I moved from there (nine years later), I had an additional two salons based across three different counties and employed 18 girls.

This huge step taught me so much.

It had been a dream come true; something I had worked so hard for and I truly felt on top of the world, a business that rewarded me both financially and emotionally, parents that were not only proud of me but also encouraged and supported me every step of the way. However, like most things, there were also many challenges. Staff sickness, lies, deceit, and a business partner who did not work as tirelessly as I did. Plus, despite my hard work to achieve its' success, clients often thought BodyMatters was part of the hairdressing company and not a separate business. At that time and for all of these reasons I felt I needed to change direction and strategy if I was going to achieve what I truly wanted for the success and freedom of BodyMatters. This was when I reached breaking point; I cut all ties with my business partner and sold off two salons leaving me with the original business I had started with.

This truly was my baby.

I took the plunge, purchased a freehold building and moved the business across town to conquer the beauty market! Our reputation was rapidly growing and, for the first time in years, I had a clear idea of who and what BodyMatters represented and what I actually wanted.

The next chapter took me to a whole new level.

My business was running smoothly, with systems in place and my wonderful, loyal staff happy. By now I was becoming bored and wanted more!

I reached out to the local college (where I had first trained as a Beauty Therapist), and was offered an opportunity to become their go-to person for bridging the gap between the educational and commercial aspects of beauty. In essence, this meant helping students become commercially ready. I remained there for five years, and even employed some outstanding students from the college in my own business.

Thirty years on, beauty is still my passion! I have always worked hard and I am still a practicing, hand's on therapist. I love the beauty industry, the clients, my staff and above all the caring industry. I have made many friends and contacts along the way, with a few detours along a sometimes, rocky road, but I still love it!

Some people might say I am a workaholic and that I live and breathe BodyMatters, but I think you do not get anywhere without hard work dedication and passion. You get out what you put in.

I love the challenge, and always encourage my staff to achieve their maximum potential and help them to fulfil their dreams.

To this day, I have staff with me who were there when I first started out.

My success story is Anna; a great therapist, once my salon manager, who only ever wanted her own business. I helped her to achieve her dreams and become successful in her own right. We have remained the best of friends; often attending courses together, working together sharing knowledge, ideas and helping each other source the best products (especially during recent months when we were hit with a pandemic).

Being a workaholic had a price. Along the way, I lost friends and my 13-year marriage sadly ended.

My wakeup call, and turning point, was falling pregnant in my early 40s. I had to take time out - I could no longer work at the drop of a hat and as I discovered, it was the best thing that happened to me. I could focus on my business not just work in it!

Returning after maternity leave, I went on a journey of self-discovery. Finding ME again the person behind all this hard work, I had proud parents and a supportive partner but had lost sight of who I was! Being a mum really does focus the mind.

Success in my eyes is all in the planning, personal development and striving for every goal you set yourself.

But ultimately, *always believe in yourself.*

It can often be very tough at the top, and very lonely but oh so rewarding. I *love* helping people to develop and achieve their goals - both staff and clients. Over the years I have been asked to talk and share my knowledge to various audiences. I appreciate these opportunities to share my experiences and always remember my late father telling me 'never miss an opportunity'!

My beauty journey has been one of discovery and consistent personal development. I cannot underestimate the importance of great communication, learning from my mistakes and working with mentors from a cross section of businesses to keep focused and forward thinking.

And I am always hungry to learn more...

I am often asked to share my success tips. Here are some of my top tips for any want-to-be salon owner:

- Treat people as you would want to be treated.

- Forge great relationships with your chosen beauty brands and suppliers. I have used Guinot since 1991 and have never looked back. I have remained loyal to this brand for many reasons; in the main they have been true to their word and supported me throughout my career.

- Know your numbers; keep an eye on your income, outgoings and profit margins. Always refer back to your business plan.

- Choose your staff carefully; your gut instinct is usually right!
  They are a key factor within your business. The right team will
  create the best environment and community; remember,
  your salon is only as good as your weakest therapist.

- Do your market and competitor research.

- Always adapt; don't be afraid to tweak or try new things.
  Take time to work ON your business, and not just in it.
  A salon is always evolving; embrace change, good and bad.

- Above all, do what you LOVE. My philosophy is: one size does
  NOT fit all. You would not call a plumber to fix your electrics.
  Stick with what you know and excel in that and be known as the
  'go to' expert.

- Look, learn and adapt. The beauty industry is always evolving,
  with new trends in the market. I have always held off, waited to see
  which trends last and importantly, researched which products or
  services would be the right fit for BodyMatters.

Since the pandemic of 2020, I have been on a journey of
personal development, and new found motivation. With
months at home I have researched, dug deep and pivoted
my business like I have never done before. Many businesses
have had to close due to the pandemic, but I have used all
that I have learnt over the years and discovered a market for
virtual beauty!

This is a very exciting development. After carefully piloting
my 30-day skincare challenge (which went down a storm)
I am now rolling this out to a wider audience... If people can
improve their fitness at home during a pandemic then why
shouldn't they improve their beauty too? But, then came the
BIG FLOOD! However I'll leave that for another time!

About Anita Stubbings

Anita has owned and operated multiple successful salons, for over 30 years. After qualifying as a Beauty Therapist in 1988, she started out in mobile beauty before working her way up to the salon owner she is today. Having perfected her craft throughout the decades, Anita has a wealth of knowledge which keeps her focused and allows her to stay true to her brand ethos of providing a natural and holistic approach to beauty.

Anita loves nothing more than helping others to fulfil their dreams and reach their true potential. She has a passion for educating and supporting future beauty therapists, focusing on the importance of them becoming commercially savvy as well as experts in the field of beauty. She is a remarkable mentor.

Despite unexpected hurdles along the way, her enthusiasm for beauty has never wavered and she has an enviable reputation as a go-to expert within the industry.

Contact Anita

bookings@bodymattersbeauty.co.uk

https://bodymattersbeauty.co.uk

https://www.facebook.com/BodyMattersBeautyTherapy

https://www.instagram.com/body_matters/?hl=en

Changing Lives!

Sandra Fludgate

I come from a family of mathematicians – apart from me – and as a pupil in the 1970s I don't remember being encouraged by school to aim for university or to even map out a career path. I did, however, manage to leave school with good exam results but without a clue as to what career I should follow. Eventually, I decided to qualify as a NNEB trained Nursery Nurse which I loved - and didn't include any maths!

After meeting the love of my life at the tender age of 17, I eventually realised that if we were to settle down, marry and buy a house that I needed to earn a little more money. So, I changed careers and began working for a distributor of electronic components even though I knew absolutely nothing about the products or the industry. Somehow, I managed to progress to the position of a Volume Pricing Coordinator managing very large accounts and negotiating orders worth up to seven-figures. I loved the job even though it was in a very male dominated industry in the 1980s and extremely stressful. Can you believe that the technology for mobile phones was in its infancy!

I did marry the love of my life at 23, we bought a house and then were very lucky to have had three fabulous sons, and I had thought my office job was stressful!

Now the one fact that I have left out so far is that I had believed since becoming a teenager that I was one of the hairiest women on the face of the earth - courtesy of my Dad. It was a constant battle trying to remain hair free. I even asked my hubby if it was like sharing the bed with a hedgehog! So, when I inherited some money, even though it could have been put to great use towards my young family, I decided this was going to be the only opportunity I was ever going to have to invest in a new treatment that I had heard about called Laser Hair Removal.

I pinned my hopes on the fact that it was going to be successful for me, that I wasn't going to regret the large expenditure, and hoped there was going to be no more spiky legs or nearly passing out during a bikini wax!

Well, how right I was... It was life changing even though the technology was in its infancy. But boy was it painful! I used to walk like John Wayne after a treatment as the skin was so sore. However, it was such a success that I became a convert, telling all my friends about this new treatment and showing them my amazing results and nice and neat bikini line! The only negative were that the treatment was very expensive and was only available in a large Medispa that had no competition, so they could charge whatever they liked.

I continued to work for the electronics industry for several years but became disheartened that my efforts only contributed to the success of someone else's business and not my own.

Around this time, I sadly lost my best friend - my Mum, who was my rock. She had run her own business successfully for many years but I knew that secretly she had always wished that she had chosen Nursing as a career. The company I worked for was subsequently bought out by an American competitor and I seized the opportunity to take redundancy.

But... what to do next??

I know. Let's retrain as a laser specialist and give *everybody* the chance to be hair free! Very random I know, but I was so sure that this was a great idea.

It's an expensive industry to enter and at that point of time was regulated by the CQC who also regulated medical practitioners, Hospitals and Dentists. I had to jump over some very high hurdles and build a business from the ground up with no prior experience of running one, no experience of the Beauty industry and a severe lack of personal funds.

However, I had passion. The passion to give other people the same life changing experience that I had experienced. A passion to be my own boss and reap my own rewards. And a passion to make my family proud of me.

Especially my Mum.

I began the business renting a room in a High Street sun bed shop. Ironic seeing as you cannot have a tan if you want laser treatments.

The first three years were very lean and sometimes very scary, especially when I arrived at work one day to find the sun bed shop had gone bankrupt and the premises were locked up with the threat of my equipment being sold to pay off their debts.

I learned many lessons along the way including that you have to believe in yourself and your services. If you give your services away for free or at a discounted price, clients will not value them either. The years of learning and practice you have put in are all part of the value.

By the fifth year I was into a healthy profit and had gained a good reputation locally for Laser Hair removal. Technology was moving on quickly with new laser systems becoming available offering many different treatments, and I had to reinvest several times to keep up-to-date with the changes.

I constantly wanted to learn and gain more qualifications, to learn about new treatments even if I didn't offer them. And I always wanted to offer the most effective treatments at an affordable price.

Research is the priority. If I was considering any new equipment or treatments I would call a clinic that were already offering the treatment - located at the other end of the country - to ask their honest opinion.

Choosing a company to supply your equipment that have the same passion about the treatments that their equipment offer, is vital. I chose a company that were science-based and not all about sales; a company who offer ongoing training as your skills improve and as new treatments become available. This would reap many rewards ensuring that I only bought the best equipment that I could afford from Lynton Lasers.

The work load eventually became too much for me on my own so I decided to relocate into a premises of my own and employ staff to fulfil the ever growing demand for my laser treatments.

I also realised that there was so much more I could offer even though I am not trained as a Beauty Therapist so employed more like minded, passionate therapists to carry out advanced treatments, too.

I now run a clinic with four qualified highly skilled therapists, who are fantastic, and this is reflected in their amazing reviews.

There are many highs and lows in running your own business and it's very hard work.

Twice I have had my business model copied by people I know, opening clinics up nearby with the same equipment and pricing. Devastating at first, but, I now prefer to see this as a compliment.

The hours are long and you have to deal with the unexpected. The pandemic of 2020 was extremely unpredictable,.

But you know, it's so very worth it when you have clients who will not go anywhere else; or who tell you how much their lives have been changed since having their treatments.

I am passionate about what I do and will be around for years to come. And that, dear reader, *is* a privilege.

About Sandra Fludgate

Sandra was born in in West London, the middle of three children. Her younger life included playing in a brass band which toured many countries and even recorded at Abbey Road Studios. Sandra is married and living in Berkshire with her husband, one old and one killer cat. She has three  sons who have carried her through adversity into success. She loves walking and green spaces which keep her sane.

As a sole trader Sandra founded *Permanent Beauty* in 2003 as a Laser Clinic that has significantly grown and now employs four therapists.

Permanent Beauty is honoured have been awarded *Berkshire's Most Trusted Clinic Award.*

Contact Sandra

permb@laser-hair.co.uk

https://permanentbeautymaidenhead.co.uk

https://www.facebook.com/PermanentBeautyMaidenhead

https://www.instagram.com/permanent_beauty_maidenhead

Never Be Afraid To Dream Big

Lesley Blair

I knew I wanted to be Chair of the British Association of Beauty Therapy and Cosmetology (BABTAC) from an early age.

My first job was as a trainee beauty therapist at Yves Rocher, I used to admire the therapists badges pinned to their uniforms - in particular their BABTAC one, I thought it looked so professional. As an impressionable 17-year-old, I asked them how I could get a badge like that and they told me it was from the leading beauty membership body in the UK and if I wanted to be respected in the industry, I should apply to join them. So, as soon as I qualified, I sent off my certificates to be verified, and was delighted when my certificate of acceptance and that coveted badge, was delivered by post. I had arrived! My certificate was signed by the Chair of the Board and I decided then that one day it would be my name.

It would take me a good 30 years to reach that point and a fair few beauty roles in between but it was always in my sights.

Despite my dad always wanting me to work in finance, I had loved the idea of working in beauty ever since I watched Grease - when Frenchie went to beauty school. Call it cliché but it seemed such a glamorous career and a job where I could both help and talk to people. Hands up, I'm a talker. My report cards would say *Lesley is such a friendly person, however if she spent as much time on her work as she does chatting, she would do a lot better.*

I see it as grounding for what I do now - being able to chat, mix with people and be social. I'm that person who goes on holiday and by the end of the first day I know everyone by the pool.

A work experience stint on the Estee Lauder counter in my local department store cemented things for me. Estee Lauder was, and remains my absolute idol. She's an icon for women, businesses and the beauty industry. When I left school and secured a job at Yves Rocher, I began training and enrolled on a youth training scheme. I got paid £26 a week and definitely had to work my way up the hard way – I was more cleaner than trainee beautician. Every day, I would go home asphyxiated by surgical spirits because I was knee deep in cleaning materials! Little did I know it would be excellent practice for when the pandemic hit.

When my year was up, I returned to Estee Lauder in a full time position. I was only 18 and flying up and down to London for training. I never let living in Scotland stop me, I just made it work. It certainly helps that I have a passion for travel. We can all put barriers in the way, but I try and find a solution. I treat business the same - never focus on the negatives, find the silver lining, admit to and learn from mistakes and then move on.

Alongside my trips to London I was doing regulated training in the evenings, weekends and my days off and after two years with Lauder, I returned to full time study and ticked off the full range of beauty qualifications - you name it, I did it.

With those under my belt, I worked in a salon, then became a mobile therapist and also began teaching.

We used to run the Confederation of International Beauty Therapy and Cosmetology (CIBTAC) exams in the college I worked for and at lunchtime the examiner would tell me of her travels to Malaysia, Singapore and the Middle East to examine CIBTAC qualifications. It sounded so exotic! By this point I had my teacher training and assessor qualifications, teaching experience and five years of industry experience so I applied and became an examiner in 1996.

For a good ten years I juggled examining internationally with building up a clientele. I rented a space in one of the nicest salons of my home town - with three rooms, a team of staff and some fabulous brands but examining got in the way as I was travelling extensively. I visited some amazing countries but at the back of my mind I was thinking about paying rent and managing staff, so I decided to give up the space and sell the business. I'm lucky enough to say that I haven't had any low points in my career, but this was a moment when I realised that I couldn't do everything and had to make a decision.

I'm from quite a high achieving family - my sister is a prosecution lawyer, and my parents built their business from scratch. My mum, who is 72 , still runs the company on her own. She is an amazing woman and inspires me daily.

Being surrounded by a strong work ethic might explain why, in my mid-30s, I decided to go back to university for four years and study a degree in Finance Investment and Risk. I'd done every job in beauty and wanted to prove to myself I could do more. On reflection I think it was a little nod and testament to my dad that I could do it, too. He passed away when he was 48, and sadly, never got to see me achieving my dreams, or to get to meet my precious nephew.

I kept my clientele and would go to lectures before and after giving treatments. To this day I still have clients from when I first qualified - I love that part of my job and could never give it up. Even when I was awarded my first-class Honours degree and had some wonderful jobs in finance at my fingertips, I just couldn't part with beauty. Instead I incorporated my degree into helping me succeed in my beauty career. Continuing to upskill is something I champion to this day. You should never give up on yourself or stop learning, sometimes we take time to reach our absolute peak in everything we are capable of.

And my peak was on its way.

In 2011, I got invited to sit on the board for BABTAC. It was an amazing moment to become part of a team that's so instrumental in advocating positive change. I was then voted to be Vice Chair and, in 2018, I fulfilled my dream and took on the role of Chair for both CIBTAC and BABTAC. I continue to treat long standing clients and do CPD when I can and that's a steady grounding. It also means I'm current and relevant when I'm writing expert reports and speaking on behalf of the industry because I'm still in the thick of it, on every level.

Without doubt, my role is a forward-facing one and while I love talking, I find public speaking nerve wracking. The first few speeches I had to make gave me nightmares for weeks in advance. With no formal training I initially found the prospect of standing in from of large groups literally terrifying.

Luckily, I am a stubborn Scot and have a *never say no* attitude.

What gets me through is that I feel genuinely honoured to represent our amazing industry. Through this past challenging year this has become an essential part of my role. I never would have believed that I would frequently be contributing to government forums, sitting on task forces meetings or being interviewed on BBC and Sky News live. While the nerves are still there I have definitely grown in confidence and proved to myself that you can achieve anything you put your mind to. If I can get the government to listen and we get results then being nervous is worth it.

It is equally important to have the courage to identify and surround yourself with people who possess skills that aren't your strength and allow them to lead when necessary. Remember, you can do anything but not everything! Teamwork and mutual respect for one another is essential for success.

On a strategic business level, both in my capacity as chair and personally, my objective is one and the same - increased regulation in beauty and national standardisation of qualifications to ensure they are fit for purpose and ultimately safeguard our customers. We are a powerful contributor to the UK economy and deserve respect.

It is therefore imperative that we are both highly professional and accountable.

The past 30 years have taught me so much but I will never stop learning – every day is a school day.

I've gone from being a naive trainee beauty therapist in Scotland to attending meetings and functions at the House of Commons, sitting on round tables with MPs, being part of All Party Parliamentary Groups (APPGs) and a member of the cosmetics intervention group for Scottish government.

Last year, I was proud and humbled to be included in the *Top 100 Beauty Influencers* by *Professional Beauty* and I have also been honoured to work closely with the other leading industry bodies as part of the government COVID taskforce. Working together with all these extraordinary industry contemporaries to help our industry overcome the challenges of the past year, while raising our sector profile within government, has been truly rewarding.

Making a difference for the greater good is what drives me. I truly believe if you persevere, the world is your oyster and you should never be afraid to dream big.

About Lesley Blair

In 2018, after 30 years in the beauty industry, Lesley Blair became Chair of both BABTAC and CIBTAC. Holding qualifications from CIBTAC, ITEC, IHBC and City & Guilds she also holds teaching, assessor and expert witness qualifications and achieved a First-Class Honours Degree in Finance in 2010. Since becoming Chair, Lesley has worked tirelessly to ensure the values and objectives of both these prominent not for profit organisations continue to be maintained, to continually raise the level of professionalism while championing fit-for-purpose qualifications.

Lesley sits on the Scottish Government's *Cosmetics Informed and Empowered Public Sub-Group JCCP Register & Stakeholder Council Steering Groups*; and contributes to the *Aesthetics and Hair & Cosmetology APPGs*. She was part of the steering group of the advanced qualifications NOS (Level 4 – 6); the *Advisory Panel of The Safety in Beauty Campaign* and the *HABIC Executive Council* (Ireland).

Through the pandemic she has worked on government task forces and inclusively with colleagues, industry bodies, and media alike for the greater good of the industry.

Contact Lesley

http://babtac.com/
https://www.linkedin.com/in/lesley-blair
Facebook: *LesleyBlair BABTAC*
Instagram: *Lesley Blair*

About Beauty Directors Club Community

Beauty Directors Club is a very unique membership for Salon, Spa and Clinic Owners.

The business world can feel like a very lonely and isolated place at times. Your family and your friends don't often understand what you are going through... but we do.

Since early in 2018, it has been an ever growing very close and supportive community, coupled with the help and advice of over ten worldwide business and personal development experts on hand whenever needed.

Beauty Directors Club has far exceeded what I thought was possible to achieve as a business resource and members have become such great friends and natural accountability partners, all around the world.

Any issue you have, then we will be there right by your side. Helping you, guiding you and supporting you at all different levels either privately or within the community.

Members have access to monthly business courses to help you stay on track with weekly mentor sessions to discuss any current issues.

There is also an amazing abundance of resources including

book downloads, meditations, workbooks and supplier discounts which are continually added to.

I look forward to meeting you and welcoming you soon.

Here's to your fantastic business success.

Susan x

susan@susanroutledge.com

http://beautydirectorsclub.com

Would You Like To Contribute To Future Editions Of Beauty And The Best?

I would like to take this opportunity to thank each and every contributor to this first edition of *Beauty And The Best*. It has been a fun, emotional and amazing process.

Beauty and The Best is written by members and close associates of the *Beauty Directors Club Community*.

If you would like to know more about the *Beauty Directors Club* and get involved in the next release of *Beauty And The Best* then please connect.

We look forward to welcoming you into our amazing community.

susan@susanroutledge.com

http://beautydirectorsclub.com